7 CHAPTERS EVERY FIRST TIME DAD NEEDS TO READ

A PREGNANCY GUIDE FOR MEN WHO DON'T HAVE
TIME TO WASTE

REMINGTON JAMES

CONTENTS

INTRODUCTION

" "*Fathering is not something perfect men do, but something that perfects the man.*"

— FRANK PITTMAN

"Do you want to hold her?" my wife asked from her hospital bed.

"I don't think that's a good idea," I answered.

I hadn't intended to say that. Until that moment when I was actually standing over my wife's bed watching her cuddle our newborn daughter, I had been looking forward to cradling my child in my arms and telling her I was her daddy. Now, standing there, I was almost petrified.

For one thing, I hadn't expected her to be so tiny. Or so wrinkled. All the newborn babies I had seen on TV were cherubic smooth-faced creatures. My daughter, born at a healthy seven pounds two ounces, wasn't that. So, I was too nervous to hold her. Suppose I squeezed her too tightly? Suppose she wriggled in a way I didn't expect, and I dropped her? Suppose she started to cry when she saw my face?

For the past eight months, after we found out that my wife Jenny was pregnant, I had been thinking about what kind of father I would be. Knowing I was going to be responsible for another human being almost overwhelmed me. I had only recently figured out how to be responsible for myself! Now I was going to be a dad. I was going to take care of another person for at least eighteen years. How would I carry that burden?

What made it worse was that I felt I had to hide these thoughts from Jenny. She had enough to deal with being pregnant, and I wanted to be the partner who made this process as easy and happy as possible. I bought two copies of *What to Expect When You're Expecting* so we could read it separately and discuss it together. I read numerous articles about how to do back massages, deal with cravings, and "active listening" during mood swings.

Most of all, I continually searched for articles about how to be a good father. I got over three billion hits on Google, most of which were written by Captain Obvious. This didn't help my confidence. If there were so few resources providing well-researched, practical advice from experts about fathering, how was I supposed to figure it out?

That's when I decided to message Roger.

We had gone to college together and had a few study groups together because we were doing the same degree. Roger was different from the other students because he was married and already had one kid. We had kept in casual touch after we graduated, mostly for professional reasons. Now I was messaging him for the most personal of reasons.

I told him I had a daughter and confessed I was already feeling overwhelmed. Did he have any advice?

"I know what you're going through," he said. "Let's meet for lunch."

As it turned out, Roger now also had a second child— his daughter was now seven, and his son was three.

"How did you manage in college?" I asked. "You were studying, working, and being a dad. I think I would have had a nervous breakdown."

"It was hard. But having a daughter actually made it easier because I knew I was doing all that for her."

"I'm worrying I'll do something that will ruin her life."

Roger chuckled. "Do you love her already?"

"I love her more than I thought I could love anybody or anything."

"Then you're on the right track. Listen, you're going to make mistakes. My children aren't in double-digit years yet, but there are already a hundred things I wish I had done differently. But they're great kids. One thing I've found out that most websites don't tell you is that children are resilient. Once we get the basics right, they'll turn out fine."

"What are the basics?" I asked, taking out my notebook.

"Seriously?" said Roger, glancing at my Mead Spiral.

"Seriously," I said, clicking my pen.

He laughed. "Okay, here goes. Pick her up when she cries, feed her when she's hungry and, when she's older, throw her in the air if she likes it and even if her mother gets nervous when you do."

"That's it?" I said.

"You'll work out the rest as you go along. Basic rule: *you* are the expert on your child, along with her mother. Read the advice from the people who studied children and parents, but always remember, none of them know your child as well as you."

I went back home feeling a lot more confident. I was a husband and a dad. These were now my most important roles in life. I had spent months learning how to best help Jenny during her pregnancy, including what to do after the baby arrived. As I would read later in *What to Expect When You're Expecting* about expectant fathers, "Some of your concerns will overlap those of mom-to-be; others will be uniquely yours. And just like your mate, you're entitled to your share of reassurance, not just during the pregnancy and the birth, but during the postpartum period as well.[1]"

Now, I was adding to my knowledge about parenting, knowing I would make mistakes but trying to make as few as possible.

One thing I soon discovered is that a lot of new Dads feel like I did. Most of us become fathers in our late 20s or early 30s. That means we're still arranging our own lives even as we bring a new little life into the world. No wonder we feel unprepared!

When Jenny fell pregnant with our son two years later, I felt a lot more prepared—both to support her during the pregnancy and help take care of the new baby. But, if you had told me before my daughter was born that I would be at ease being home by myself with a baby, I would have laughed in your face (or, maybe, thrown up).

Looking back, I took as much delight in the births of both my children, but I have to admit that I took a lot more pleasure in caring for my son. By the time he came along, I had already read most of the research you will find in this book. I also had two years of experience in infant care I could now put toward my son. Just as importantly, I was now more in sync as a parent with my partner. Our nerves were lezz frazzled. We didn't have to work out who was doing what or spend so much time working out our schedules.

Most importantly, the second time around, we both got more sleep and more sex, this time at the same time (. . . don't ask).

If you're picking up this book, it's most likely because you feel, as I once did, just totally lost at sea. Fatherhood is still an unknown ocean because, until about fifteen years ago, most parenting studies only had mothers and their children as subjects. "Fathers are vastly important in their children's lives, in ways that both scholars and parenting experts have overlooked," notes science writer Paul Raeburn in his book *Do Fathers Matter?*[2]

Even though the experts have ignored this, I believe many men know this. We want to be good fathers. We want our children to love us. We don't want to be among the set of men who, if we get divorced from our wives, we also get divorced from our children. The most unsung heroes of the Gen X and millennial generations are those fathers who raised well-balanced children while maintaining strong relationships with their spouses.

Even so, I found that, although it's not easy to come by, there's a wealth of information out there that can help us make the journey, if not easy, at least less difficult. I wrote this book to hopefully make your experience a little easier than mine. Some of the questions I discovered that nearly all new fathers have are:

- How do I help my partner during pregnancy?
- How will our relationship be affected by the baby?
- How can I ease the child-caring burden for my partner?
- What fathering style is best for children?
- How do I balance work and parenting?

This book will help you understand what your partner is going through during pregnancy and provide strategies on how to take care of her and your baby before, during, and after childbirth so you'll have a healthy and happy family. For instance, most couples think their relationship will become stronger with the arrival of a baby. This is generally true in the long term but, in those first few months (or, sometimes, years), marriages take a pounding. As scientist John Medina notes in his book *Brain Rules for Baby*, the new parents experience four main sources of conflict: (1) sleep loss, (20 social isolation, (3) unequal workload, and (4) depression[3].

Had I read all this material before Jenny became pregnant and before my daughter was born, I would have saved myself a lot of worry (and also not wasted so many diapers). Not only do I present the most reliable research, but I also provide practical tips I've gleaned through both reading and my own experience as a new dad.

I can virtually guarantee that, by the end of this book (and with some practice), you will be ready to face all the important challenges that a new baby brings. Most importantly, though, this book explores how to think about your role as a dad—what that means, how it changes your life, and how you lay the foundations for a relationship with your child that will last a lifetime.

1

START WITH SUPPORT

This chapter tells you what you can do to support your pregnant partner and prepare for your baby's needs before birth.

Having gotten her pregnant, you've probably been feeling like a man—a real man. Now you know you make your own people. That's good. You'll need that mindset to face the challenges of being a real husband and a real father. Luckily, these first stages are what you, as a male, were built for.

How so? Because a lot of the most useful things you can do during pregnancy and your baby's first months involve (1) researching stuff, (2) making lists, and (3) getting what's on those lists.

Take, for instance, research. Men, generally speaking, are all about facts. Even boys who read prefer factual books (types of dinosaurs, models of cars, famous murderers). We don't feel comfortable tackling any challenge unless we have information, which is why we often don't feel comfortable about feelings. And, since pregnancy tends to make her awash with emotions, we'll have to deal with that, too. (Don't worry: I got you covered.)

Then there are the lists. Men tend to be more enthused about lists than women (except grocery lists, which is why we always forget some item she wanted us to get or, worse, get shredded cheddar cheese when she wanted grated parmesan cheese). This chapter provides the research so you don't have to do it yourself and also the list of things you need to acquire and do.

I suggest you write down, photograph, or screenshot these lists. Even before you start shopping, just having the lists in your pocket will make you feel more prepared and organized—which, if you're obsessive-compulsive like me, is the exact same thing.

The lists are also important because they prove your continued importance as a dad, which seems doubtful nowadays in certain circles. (I won't name the circles, but I will say that a lot of the people in them are shaped like one.) From an evolutionary perspective, human males were once absolutely essential to the birthing process. After all, in prehistoric days, a pregnant woman was vulnerable to both predators and nature. She could not wield a weapon effectively, run fast, or climb. She was limited in her ability to gather food. So, she needed the protection of a man.

These conditions no longer exist in our modern society but, despite all the hype of mothers doing it all on their own, a pregnant woman or a mother who lacks male support still has more challenges than a woman with a spouse, and I don't mean just opening jars. You will see this for yourself when you realize how much help you can give your partner. However, before we get into those practicalities, let's cover the information basics about pregnancy. The more you know about pregnancy, the more you'll be able to support your partner throughout the pregnancy and birth.

20 Things Nobody Tells You about Pregnancy and Parenthood

Before we get down and rather dirty, here are some key things you need to know. I'll be expanding on some of these points later in the book.

1. Once the baby comes, your life will never be the same. That's a good thing.
2. The first sign of pregnancy isn't necessarily morning sickness—it's your partner's sense of smell getting so sensitive that she can moonlight helping the police track escaped convicts. Warning to you: bathe three times a day, and don't cheat.
3. Don't make any comments about how much she's eating or what she's eating
4. Forget timing the contractions. Just have the go-bag ready for when your wife/spouse announces it's time.
5. When going to the hospital, make sure your cellphone and Kindle are fully charged and carry a power bank or three.
6. Whether you go to the delivery room or not depends on whether your wife really wants you there or really does not and whether you get scared by horror movies.
7. Unless you're related to Warren Buffet, say goodbye to disposable cash. You won't buy beer, a new iPhone, or that cordless power drill with a solar battery you would never have used anyway.
8. You *will* buy that stroller with the extra cupholders, built-in food container, and

automatic collapsible button. Ditto crib, bassinet, and stuff to hang on them that will help your baby develop their cognitive abilities. (Note: they're called a crib mobile, and at best, they entertain your child but won't turn them into Baby Einstein.)

9. Once the baby is home, you will be living on canned food, TV dinners, and home delivery, depending on how much you've spent on the stroller, bassinet, crib, etc.

10. Breast is best, but formula won't ruin your baby's future.

11. You will not get a full night's sleep for at least a month . . . At least. You will discover how much you need a full night's sleep. You will learn to function without a full night's sleep.

12. Nothing will fascinate you more than your newborn baby. You will be able to spend hours watching their toes.

13. Yes, men can change diapers. And, if your baby is a boy, you will change them better than your wife because you know how to dodge pee.

14. You will not be disgusted by your baby's spit-up, throw-up, or even poop. Seriously. Which is useful because you'll be wiping their butts for about two to three years.

15. Your mother and other people will tell you not to spoil your baby by picking them up every time they cry since this will make them too clingy.
16. Pick up your baby every time they cry.
17. You will begin to view childless people as a different species of human. Try not to display your contempt for them.
18. Don't talk too much to other people about your baby because nobody finds your baby as interesting as you do except your wife. And maybe not even her.
19. Don't expect sex and, even if you get some, it won't be the exciting kind.
20. After weeks of not having any time alone, you and your partner will get a babysitter and go out and find yourself missing the baby. You will also call the babysitter too often.

This is your baby in her belly[1]

"Natal" means "of or relating to the place or time of one's birth, and "pre" means "before." So "prenatal" is all about what happens when the baby is still inside the woman's womb.

Now, even if you know little or nothing about prenatal development, you may have some vague notion that the mother-to-be must eat right and remain unstressed if she and you are to have a healthy, happy baby. And you're probably worried about ensuring she gets everything she craves and that you don't make her so stressed out that something happens to the fetus.

So, here's the first thing you need to do: put all those ideas out of your head!

Once you're past the first three months, the fetus is pretty tough. A pregnant woman has to be virtually starving or under extreme and continual stress for the fetus to be affected. That doesn't mean she mustn't make every effort to eat nutritious food and stay calm. But neither you nor her should worry about getting every detail exactly right.

If you need to worry, it's in the first 12 weeks. This is when the risk of miscarriage is highest—more accurately, least low since just 15 percent of all pregnancies end in miscarriage[2]—and when she'll be experiencing morning sickness (which can also happen in the evening, at night, and at high noon). Pregnancy lasts approximately 40 weeks. So, let's go through the major milestones.

Prenatal development happens in three stages:

- Germinal stage: Weeks #1 and #2 after conception
- Embryonic stage: Weeks #3 through #8
- Fetal stage: after Week #9

At the germinal stage, the fertilized egg is called a zygote. The zygote first divides into two cells, then into four, and continues doubling. But from eight cells, differentiation occurs, which is to say that the cells already begin specializing in forming the various parts that will become your baby. This next stage is called a blastocyst, which is made up of three layers[1]: the ectoderm (skin and nervous systems), the endoderm (digestive and respiratory systems), and the mesoderm (muscle and skeletal systems).

The blastocyst has to attach itself to the uterine wall, a process called implantation. This is when things get real. Once implantation is successful, the woman starts experiencing hormonal changes.

At that point, you need to start upping your game. She may start having nausea, and her sense of smell gets so acute that you had better make sure your feet are pristine. Her womb now has an embryo that looks more or less like a tadpole. The head starts to form around the fourth week, then the features—eyes, nose, ears, and mouth—follow in short order. Arms and leg buds form in the following week and, by Week #8, all the basic organs are in place, except the sex organs. (It's too early for that and, especially if your baby is a girl, you'll discover that even seventeen years is too early for sex organs.)

Week #6 or so is the second most important one in the embryo's life. That's when the brain and nervous system begin to form—in other words, the person who will become your child.

Once cell differentiation is complete, the embryo becomes a fetus. Between Week #9 and Week #12, the fetus begins moving its arms and legs. Your partner won't feel kicks till about Weeks #16 to #25. Around the latter week, sex organs also start forming and, contrary to what you hear on the sports news nowadays, these determine whether you're going to have a girl or a boy. (The default sex of the fetus is female, by the way—it takes an additional hormonal signal to grow the testicles and penis.)

Most of the fetus's growth is later in the pregnancy, and why some women's stomachs seem to go from basketball to beach ball overnight.

Birth of a Dad

If you're really nervous about becoming a father, taking a birthing class can do a lot to ease your fears (or, as we've experienced, dads like to call it, terror).

As a father of three, Andy Shaw puts it on his <u>blog Insta Father</u>, "I needed to get some confidence. And these classes, especially the main one, did just that. I learned so much it was ridiculous, from ways to soothe the baby to what to expect at childbirth, including what the baby really will look like—the 'newborn baby' you see on TV is likely a 3-month-old because a bluish, sticky baby isn't as cute. The class was a *huge* confidence booster as a new dad[3]."

Andy recommends that you and your partner choose a birthing class together. Bear in mind that different instructors will have different approaches, so you need to choose someone who's in sync with you as a couple. So, before you go asking around, make sure you're clear on the following:

- Your birthing plan (what arrangements and procedures you prefer).
- What kind of information you want (about labor only, or also postdelivery issues such as baby care?).

- Preferred size of the class (small gets you more personalized attention, but big means more people to have discussions with).
- What class times fit your schedule (including whether they offer online options).
- What learning styles you prefer (visual, auditory, or kinesthetic, role play, art, etc.).
- What materials you'll be getting (written, DVDs, audio tapes).
- Whether you want a class that focuses on father-to-be or both parents (some instructors see Dad as a helper or bystander rather than central to the process—you *definitely* don't want them telling you what to do).

Let's go into more detail about your birthing plan [4] since this will mainly determine what you want to get out of a birthing class. The birth plan should include whatever information you and your partner have decided is important. Needless to say, what she says goes since she's the one delivering the baby. The plan should also be approved by your gynecologist/obstetrician, even if they're not the ones doing the actual delivery. You should also make copies to give to the nurses and the postnatal team.

The plan should cover all or some of the following issues:

1. Whether your partner wants you (or somebody else) in the delivery room with her.
2. Whether she can eat or drink during labor.
3. Whether a water birth in a tub is preferred.
4. What birthing position she prefers.
5. Whether the delivery room should have music and/or lighting she has chosen.
6. Whether the birth will be recorded and, if so, who will do it.
7. Whether she wants a natural delivery or a C-section.
8. What pain medication or pain relief technique she wants.
9. Whether the delivery team will cut or allow natural tearing if required.
10. Helping labor with drugs or not.
11. Use of equipment such as forceps or vacuum to assist in the delivery.
12. Whether she prefers to hold the baby right after birth to crawl to the breast or have it taken away to be cleaned, etc.
13. Spending some time with the baby before he or she is weighed and checked by the delivery team.

14. Whether the team should cut the placenta cord or her partner.

A birthing class should address all these issues and help you streamline the plan. In all this, however, you should keep in mind the old military principle: "All plans die on the battlefield." While most deliveries go smoothly, something might happen that makes it impossible to meet your partner's preferences if she and the baby are to be safe and healthy. Birth, like parenthood, means always expecting the unexpected when you're expecting. (But, as a man, you know this is true even for women who aren't pregnant.)

What the baby needs (and doesn't)[5]

Now we get into the nitty-gritty hardcore stuff of baby care: diapers and other unfamiliar things. Let's start with a short list of what you'll need for the first three months after baby comes. (Yes, the following is actually a short list.)

Baby essentials for the first three months

- Car seat—and make sure you don't put it behind the driver's seat.
- Onesies—you thought they were cute before? But don't buy too many of one size because your baby is going to grow faster than you think.
- Baby sleepers or sleep sacks—no, they won't help you get more sleep.
- Baby socks—not to be used with onesies.
- Newborn hats, depending on climate—be prepared for your gangsta baby.
- Disposable diapers or cloth diapers (and detergent for washing)—big difference in time and effort. Also, buy more than you think a baby could possibly go through in a week.
- Disposable wipes or twelve cloth wipes—I didn't even know there were cloth wipes before I saw this list, and I still haven't seen one.
- Diaper rash cream—actually works.
- Waterproof pad for diaper changes—get three.
- Diaper pail or receptacle—preferably with a foot pedal or even an automatic sensor.
- Baby washcloths—will be used for more than three months.

- Hooded towels—you'll be taking quite a few photos when they're wearing this.
- Baby sponge—this is actually just for the first three weeks when you'll do sponge baths instead of in the bathtub. But you don't need to do this every day. Only the butt gets dirty.
- Baby bath wash—a lot easier than soap.
- Baby lotion—if "smoother than a baby's skin" isn't true, what do you need lotion for?
- Baby bathtub—buy it larger than you think you need.
- Baby nail clippers—yes, you will actually need those if you don't want people to think you live with a demented cat.
- Digital thermometer—underarm also works just fine. Get one that beeps when the temperature is taken.
- Medicine dropper.
- Bulb syringe/nasal aspirator—or you can do it the old-fashioned way and suck the snot out of their nose.
- Crib, cradle, or bassinet—you'll enjoy choosing these just because of the various gadgets.
- Fitted sheets and mattress cover for crib, cradle, or bassinet.
- Burp cloths—the polite name for cloths to catch vomit.

- Bottles, if you're bottle-feeding, and bottle brush—get these even if you're not bottle-feeding. Seriously.
- A variety of bottle nipples in different sizes—your baby will choose which one he or she likes.
- Breastfeeding pillow, nursing pads, and nipple cream—let your wife choose all of these.
- Breast pump—as above.

Breast is best, but . . .

If your partner is <u>breastfeeding</u>, you have all the equipment you need. But, more often than not, you want to have formula and baby bottles on standby. That also means having something to boil the bottles in because sterilization is key when you're bottle-feeding. Will using formula lower your baby's IQ or make them fat? <u>The short answer is "No"</u>[6]. Studies that claim otherwise have used flawed methodologies, such as comparing breastfed babies from one cohort to formula-fed babies from another. This means that a whole range of other factors besides feeding could explain different outcomes. <u>One study</u> that compared siblings who had been either breastfed or formula-fed found no significant differences in key metrics[7].

If you plan on formula feeding, try different brands if the first doesn't agree with your baby. You'll also need to use different-sized nipples (the size of the hole) to find out which one they're most comfortable with.

Where should your baby sleep?

Here are your four options: (1) in another room, (2) in the same room with you and your partner, or (3) in the same bed as both of you, (4) in a different state than you (yes, there will be moments when you wish that).

The <u>American Academy of Pediatrics</u> recommends that "parents sleep in the same room—but not in the same bed as a baby, preferably for at least the first six months[8]." Many American parents seem to think that putting the baby in a separate room will help them become independent in later life. But we did not evolve to be alone in our first few years—given the threat of predators, very much the opposite. A baby who wakes up alone immediately gets stressed. Additionally, having the baby in the same room allows the parents to hear and respond to any sounds of distress more quickly. And, despite what the AAP says, co-sleeping is more common than not in most cultures. In her book *Parenting Without Borders*, journalist Christine Gross-Loh writes, "In a study of 136 societies, infants sleep in beds with their mothers in two-thirds of the communities . . . Out of 100 countries in another survey, only

American parents had a separate sleeping space for their children[9]."

If you're worried about rolling over on your baby, you can get a "sleep nest"—a sleeper with raised sides small enough to fit on the bed (assuming you have a queen- or king-sized bed). The big advantage of co-sleeping is that nobody has to get up when the baby needs to be breastfed or just comforted. Just make sure to use waterproof bedding, although diaper leaks really shouldn't happen if you've put them on right.

Ten ways to support your pregnant partner[10]

The website I got these suggestions from originally had fifteen ways, but I didn't want to be too ambitious. While I thought most of the points were good (not the stuff about pillows and running her a bath), I also didn't always agree with how those points should be executed. So, choose what works for you and ignore what doesn't.

1. *Help without being asked.* That means housework. She's pretty much going to be tired every day for forty weeks. So, you have to step up. That also means finding out *how* to do the chores she usually does, as in "How do you like the dishes washed, babe?" and "How should I

mop/vacuum?" and "How will I know when the floor is clean?"

2. *Get informed.* Which is exactly what you're doing by reading this book. Excellent start! Also, talk to your friends with kids, your dad, and also your divorced friends (so you'll know what *not* to do).

3. *Be there.* Time to put down the game console and give up YouTube, Twitter, and Instagram (at least while she's awake). Go to the doctor's visits with her as often as possible, and every time when they're doing an ultrasound. If she's taking antenatal classes, take them with her. Have many baby discussions. Feel her belly.

4. *Let her know she's beautiful.* But don't exaggerate, and don't lie. Some women look terrible when pregnant. The point is, let her know you find her to be pregnant-beautiful because she's carrying your child.

5. *Give massages.* You like getting those, and you're not even pregnant. Besides, giving her lots of massages will help preserve that sensual connection for when it's time for you both to have sex again. (More on that in Chapter Seven if you want to skip ahead.)

6. *Be understanding.* If she seems to get crazy during this period, like crying copiously

because the tomatoes got squishy, just comfort her and promise to get her firmer tomatoes.

7. *Listen.* It may be that her sole topic of conversation is about her body, what the baby is doing, and what he or she will do. Don't interrupt her to discuss the latest trending topic on Twitter, the mix-up with accounts receivables at work, or the ethical implications of Hume's self-ownership. Best responses: "Hm," "I see," "True," punctuated by encouraging nods.

8. *Talk about it.* If she does run out of breath, you can then express some of the same concerns. Don't say anything too heavy on her, though. She doesn't want to be taking care of two babies.

9. *Prioritize her.* Since you're probably getting less sex or none at all, she may be worrying that you're losing interest in her. Also, she feels less attractive, and she knows she's being moodier. So, give a few extra hugs and kisses and, at least once or twice a month, watch a chick flick with her. (Not the movie *What to Expect When You're Expecting*, though—Dennis Quaid will just make you feel inadequate.)

10. *Create some memories.* When baby comes, that's the end of life as you knew it. You won't even

be able to leave the house without making a plan first. So, use these last months to go to the movies, drive through the countryside, and spend the weekend at a hotel. Talk a lot about how you met, what you liked about her, and how your first date went. All this will reassure her about your relationship in the coming months. Also, take photos of *everything*, especially her belly.

Those ten acts should get you valuable partner points. But here's what will really clinch your dad-to-be credentials: go to Human Resources and get all the required information about insurance coverage for the delivery and parental leave. Also, draw up a baby budget and, if it looks good, show it to her. Back in the day, all you had to do was kill an antelope to get in good with your woman. This is the modern equivalent.

Now, since you've stepped up to take care of her emotional needs, the next chapter should be a relative breeze: taking care of your partner's physical well-being.

HELPING HER STAY HEALTHY DURING PREGNANCY

I f you want your baby to be healthy, start by helping your pregnant partner achieve a healthy lifestyle. It's like building a strong foundation for your child's health.

In this chapter, you will learn about your partner's health care needs during pregnancy, including proper nutrition, foods to avoid, exercise, and how to get important information from your visits to the doctor for prenatal tests.

Before we get into all that, though, let me caution you on two mistakes I made that, if your partner is less tolerant than my Jenny was, may end up with you getting divorced before your child is even born.

Because I am obsessed with information, I read up on everything I could about pregnancy, especially health issues. That was my first mistake. There were so many problems, apparently, that could arise if you didn't eat the right foods, take the right vitamins, and exercise on most days for most of the nine months or even before. Your baby might come out underweight, overweight, lose some IQ points, cry too much, cry too little, have a heart attack when they're forty, and maybe become a serial killer.

As a result of my own fears, I ended up trying to control what she was eating, nagging her about getting enough exercise, and even (this was my biggest mistake) cautioning her about gaining too much weight.

"Why, Remy?" she asked sweetly. "Does this pregnancy make me look fat?"

She should have clouted me across the head, but she's a forgiving wife.

So, my first caution is: Don't panic about your partner's health. Most of the pregnancy information on the internet is scary—and that's by design. After all, these websites want to get clicks so they can get advertisers, and scaring vulnerable people—and a pregnant woman is the most vulnerable kind of human—is an effective way to do this.

This doesn't mean that the information these websites provide is unreliable. But the advice is often presented in a way to make you worry. Here, I provide information as objectively as possible.

My second caution is: Don't force anything on your spouse. Even in normal circumstances, getting another person to eat right and exercise regularly is almost impossible unless they already want to. When a woman is pregnant, she will have cravings, and she will often be too tired to work out. But, remember, she's carrying the baby. She's far more motivated than you to do the right things.

So, your only role is to support her in that. You have to go out and buy the healthy foods and snacks—and eat them, too. You can't be devouring a juicy cheeseburger if she can't have one. And, if you want her to get more exercise, you have to be there working out right alongside her.

With that out of the way, let's start with the first step in pregnancy health: the prenatal visit.

Before baby

The main reason for prenatal checkups is to identify problems before they happen and, if any do occur, to deal with them early[1].

You will be going to one of the following health practitioners for her prenatal visits:

- Obstetrician—these are doctors who specialize in pregnancy and childbirth.
- Obstetricians/gynecologists (OB/GYNs)—they specialize in pregnancy, childbirth, and women's health.
- Family (or general) practitioner—these doctors are not specialists but deal with a range of health issues for all types of patients, including prenatal care.
- Nurse or midwife—these practitioners specialize in women's health care, including prenatal care, labor and delivery, along with postpartum care after a normal delivery.
- Most women prefer to go with a specialist, but this is really only necessary if they have some risk factors, such as diabetes, hypertension, or obesity. It's also better to go with an OB/GYN if you fall into the following categories:
- thirty-five or older
- increased risk of preterm labor
- carrying twins
- any other complications that put you in a high-risk category

But, no matter what kind of practitioner you choose, the decisive factor should be comfort. You want somebody who gives you and your partner the kind of attention and care you deserve throughout the pregnancy. One caveat is that the nurse or midwife and even the GP have to call in a doctor if a C-section is planned for delivery or becomes necessary during labor. So, shop around before you decide who's best for both of you (and baby makes three).

What happens during a prenatal visit?

Once you're healthy and have no risk factors, your partners (and, preferably, you as well) will be visiting your health care provider every four weeks until Week #28 of the pregnancy. After that, visits will be once a fortnight until Week #36 and then every week until delivery.

Or not.

The fact is, once the pregnancy is proceeding as normal, you can save money by spacing out these visits. Counterintuitively, the final visits after Week #36 are the least necessary because, if any problems were to occur, they would have most likely happened already.

So, here's what happens on these visits:

- Weight and blood pressure are taken.
- Size and shape of the uterus are checked.
- Ultrasound is done to see whether the fetus is growing and developing normally (usually started by Week #22).
- Urine test is done for sugar (diabetes, usually done at Week #24) and protein (kidney function).

If your doctor believes you might be at risk for gestational diabetes, they will test you at Week #12. Your partner is at higher risk of this if (1) they previously had a baby that weighed more than nine pounds (4.1 kilograms), (2) have a family history of diabetes, and (3) are obese (more than 50 lbs/22.6 kg overweight).

Then there are theprenatal tests. These are done to see if there's a birth defect or a chromosomal problem in the fetus. Some are screening tests designed to reveal a possible issue, while others are diagnostic tests (blood tests, amniocentesis, CVS, and ultrasound exams) that are meant to find specific issues. All these tests are done in the first, second, and third trimesters.

What you decide to do in the unlikely event a problem is discovered is up to your partner and you. But even if terminating the pregnancy is not on the cards, you should still do these tests. That way, your doctor can be prepared for any delivery issues, and you will also be ready emotionally for the challenges.

I want to emphasize, though, that this is not something you should worry about too much. The overall rate of babies born with birth defects is <u>3 in every 100</u>[2], and even that rate is exaggerated since it's women with health issues who account for most such births.

I also want to mention something I only found out after our first child was born—that ultrasounds may affect the fetus. One 2011 study found "a statistically significant—albeit weak—association between ultrasound screening during pregnancy and being non-right-handed later in life[3]."

Since nine out of ten people are right-handed, ultrasounds may possibly affect the wiring of the fetal brain within the womb. Our daughter is happy and healthy, but some couples may want to limit the ultrasounds to only key milestones in the pregnancy—maybe three or four in total. We did so for our second child, who's also healthy and happy.

Don't worry, be informed

However, there are some concerns that even healthy pregnant women should be aware of. These include:

Preeclampsia (also called toxemia of pregnancy): This condition can happen around the sixth month of pregnancy. It causes high blood pressure, edema (fluid buildup that causes the hands, feet, and face to swell), and protein in the urine.

Rh-negative mother/Rh-positive fetus (also called Rh incompatibility): This is an element that everyone has in their blood, which can be positive or negative, just as you can have O-positive or O-negative blood. If the fetus is Rh-positive, but you're Rh-negative, your body reacts by making antibodies that can destroy the fetus's red blood cells. This is a potential issue, but it's also a manageable one. According to KidsHealth, "Rh incompatibility usually isn't a problem if it's the mother's first pregnancy. That's because the baby's blood does not normally enter the mother's circulatory system during the pregnancy[4]."

Diet and Weight Gain

So, this is the elephant in the room (and definitely don't use that phrase with your partner). Here are your targets for your partner: if she's normal weight, she should try to gain about 25–35 pounds (11.3–15.8 kilograms) during her pregnancy. If she's overweight when she falls pregnant, she shouldn't gain more than 15–25 pounds (6.8–11.3 kilograms). And, if she's underweight, she needs to put on between 28 to 40 pounds (12.7–18.1 kilograms).

Tip: let the health care professional tell her whether she's overweight or underweight. You stay out of it. Way out. Your job is to help her put on the right amount of weight by calculating how many calories she needs per day and getting healthy foods to do so. Basically, she will need to add about 300 calories to her normal daily diet, all of which will be consumed by the baby growing inside her. The focus should be on protein but also include lots of fresh fruits, grains, and vegetables.

Your health care professional may also recommend supplements such as iron, calcium, and folic acid, the first two because the fetus will be drawing on your body to build its own body, and the last one to prevent neural tube defects. For the first two, both of you should monitor her physiological reactions (does her stool get hard, her fingernails too white?) to determine how much she should take. However, folic acid is a must-take since it helps prevent spina bifida.

You'll want to make sure she's eating foods that provide these extra minerals. Go to the greengrocers regularly! The table below lists what you should get:

Iron	Calcium
red meat	Milk
dark poultry	pasteurized cheese
salmon	Yogurt
Eggs	orange juice
Tofu	Tofu
enriched grains	soy milk
dried beans and peas	dried beans
dried fruits	Almonds
dark leafy green vegetables	spinach, kale, and broccoli
iron-fortified breakfast cereals	calcium-fortified cereals

You can also print out the following food chart that shows what you should get/cook for her during each month of her pregnancy. But remember the Golden Pregnancy Rule: her body decides what it wants.

Source: NourishedNaturalHealth

Here's some detailed information that will help you buy or prepare nutritious non-vomit meals for her.

Dairy products. These contain two types of high-quality protein: casein and whey. Dairy is the best dietary source of calcium and also has good things like phosphorus, B vitamins, magnesium, and zinc.

Legumes. These include lentils, peas, beans, chickpeas, soybeans, and peanuts. They provide fiber, protein, iron, folate, and calcium, which her fetus is greedy for. You can add legumes to her diet with meals like hummus on whole grain toast or black beans in a taco salad.

Sweet potatoes. These are rich in beta-carotene, which is a source of vitamin A, an essential vitamin for fetal development. It also has a lot of fiber, which helps with constipation.

Salmon. Excellent source of omega-3 fatty acids, which have all kinds of health benefits, and a natural source of vitamin D for strong bones and a robust immune system. Up your culinary (or credit card) skills by offering her smoked salmon, grilled salmon, or cooked in some kind of non-wine sauce. Serve with bagels, rice, pasta, vegetables, or all of the above.

Eggs. Eggs are, without exaggeration, the ultimate health food. They have pretty much every nutrient you need—80 calories, high-quality protein, fat, and many vitamins and minerals. For your pregnant partner, the choline in eggs is a vital nutrient for baby's brain development and for preventing developmental abnormalities of the brain and spine. Also, there are a few hundred ways to cook and prepare eggs, so she must like at least one of them, hopefully.

Broccoli and dark, leafy greens. Provide fiber, vitamin C, vitamin K, vitamin A, calcium, iron, folate, and potassium. If she doesn't like them by themselves, use them as ingredients.

Lean meat and proteins. Beef and pork provide iron, choline, and other B vitamins—all of which she needs more of during pregnancy. Low iron levels during early and mid-pregnancy can lead to iron deficiency anemia, which increases the risk of low birth weight. To help with iron absorption, prepare dishes that combine iron-rich foods with food that have vitamin C, such as tomatoes.

Berries. Provide her with healthy carbs, vitamin C, fiber, and antioxidants. They're a great snack because they have both water and fiber and are nutritious with fewer calories. So, stock up on blueberries, raspberries, goji berries, strawberries, and acai berries.

Whole grains. These include oats, quinoa, brown rice, wheat berries, and barley. Whole grains have fiber and vitamins. Some, like oats and quinoa, also provide protein and magnesium, all of which are good for pregnant women.

Avocado. Avocados are the pregnancy fruit par excellence. The fruit's healthy fats help build the skin, brain, and tissues of the fetus. Avocados are high in <u>monounsaturated fatty acids</u> (i.e., healthy fats), fiber, B vitamins, potassium, copper, and vitamins E, K, and C. The avocado's creamy texture makes a wonderful spread (add salt and black pepper, maybe some garlic powder) or a sliced side dish. You can use it as guacamole, in salads, in smoothies, and on whole wheat toast, but also as a substitute for mayo or sour cream.

Dried fruit. These include prunes and dates. They have the same amount of nutrients as fresh fruit and are high in calories, fiber, vitamins, and minerals. <u>Prunes</u> are rich in fiber, potassium, and vitamin K, while <u>dates</u> have fiber, potassium, and iron.

Fish liver oil. This provides omega-3 fatty acids EPA and DHA, which are essential for fetal brain and eye development. Fish liver oil may also help prevent premature delivery. And all she needs to take is one tablespoon every day or three, depending on how she reacts.

What does Captain Obvious say?

He says, "Don't smoke, drink, or take drugs, kids." Also, get enough sleep.

Try to avoid over-the-counter medicines since they may affect the fetus. Get a list of what your health care professional considers safe, including natural remedies. "Natural" is NOT a synonym for "safe."

Here are some of the physical changes you might see in your partner. Depending on her personality (and your acting ability), either pretend not to notice or assure that she looks even better. Possible changes:

- leg swelling
- <u>varicose veins</u> in the legs and the area around the vaginal opening
- hemorrhoids
- heartburn and constipation
- backache
- sleep loss

You can assist your partner with some of these issues by putting her in the right sleep position. Lying on her side can prevent or reduce varicose veins, hemorrhoids, and swollen legs. This also prevents the fetus from putting pressure on the large blood vessels that carry blood to her heart and lungs, hence putting less work on her heart. If you put her on her left side, this assists blood flow to the placenta.

You can also make her more comfortable by propping pillows between her legs, behind her back, and underneath her belly.

Just make sure you find out whether she wants to be woken up to shift or prefers to sleep in the 'wrong' position, and then go along with whatever she says.

(Some) foods are your enemy, and your body will tell you so

Have you ever wondered why women get morning sickness when they're pregnant? Probably not, since you're a man and will never face that problem. Anyway, turns out there's a reason for it: when a woman becomes pregnant, her brain gets hypersensitive to toxic elements, which luckily don't include your masculinity.

This is why her sense of smell becomes so acute. Any foods with even the slightest trace of toxins trigger her vomit reflex. And it turns out that women who have morning sickness are less likely to have miscarriages than women who have a nausea-free pregnancy[5].

Thus, your job as the male partner is to list those foods and make sure you don't eat them—if you do, do so at least a mile away and brush your teeth and use mouth-wash afterward. If, however, your partner is not experiencing morning sickness, it might be a good idea to ensure she doesn't eat the below foods, which are known to cause illnesses like <u>listeriosis</u> and toxoplas-mosis. These can result in birth defects or miscarriages. So, steer clear of the following:

- "fresh" (i.e., unpasteurized) cheeses (such as feta, goat, Brie, Camembert, and blue cheese)
- raw milk
- fresh juices, including apple cider
- raw eggs or foods containing raw eggs, such as mousse and tiramisu
- undercooked meats, fish, or shellfish

You can and should eat fish and shellfish, but there are certain species you need to avoid because they have high concentrations of mercury—a chemical that can damage your fetus's brain. Fish to avoid include shark, swordfish, king mackerel, marlin, tuna (bigeye or ahi), and tilefish.

Make sure she has a good supply of lean meats, fruits, vegetables, and whole-grain breads.

Working out the workout

First rule: it's up to her how much exercise she does and whether she does any at all. You're not the one carrying around a steadily growing kettlebell in your tummy. What you can do is make sure you're there to help her exercise if she decides to do so.

If your spouse is fitness-inclined, show her the <u>potential benefits</u> of continuing her workout routine[6]. These include weight control, mood control (which benefits you, too), and an easier labor when that time comes (there's a reason it's called "labor"). Regular workouts during pregnancy also reduce the risks of hypertension and pre-eclampsia.

Here's a list of other benefits:

- increased energy
- improved fitness
- reduced back and pelvic pain
- fewer complications in delivery
- faster recuperation after labor
- prevention and management of urinary incontinence
- improved posture
- improved circulation
- stress relief

- reduced risk of anxiety and depression
- improved sleep and management of insomnia
- increased ability to cope with the physical demands of motherhood (and fatherhood)

Make sure you both consult your doctor or physiotherapist to discuss what kind of exercises she can and cannot do. It will be useful to do a pre-exercise screening to identify any physical conditions that might make exercise during pregnancy risky for her or the fetus.

She also needs to be cautious about some things because her body is changing while she's pregnant. For instance, pregnancy hormones, such as the aptly named "relaxin," loosen her ligaments. This will help her adapt to the growing weight in her womb and also during labor, but it also puts her at greater risk of joint injuries.

Also, since pregnancy increases her resting heart rate, she mustn't use that measure to calculate the desired exertion rate. She shouldn't let her heart rate go above 75 percent of her maximum rate, so you can monitor that for her during her workout. She has to be in tune with her body and decide when enough is enough. You can help by observing her during her routine.

Her blood pressure drops in the second trimester, meaning she should not change positions rapidly, as happens during a workout and sex, since this can cause dizziness.

So, what does a good pregnancy exercise routine look like? You can become her exercise coach.

If your partner isn't already fit, both of you start off with low-intensity exercises such as walking or light weights. This can start with 15 minutes per day and build up to longer sessions.

Other moderate exercises include:

- swimming
- cycling
- jogging
- aquarobics
- yoga
- Pilates

If she exercised regularly before getting pregnant, you could start with at least 30 minutes of moderate to intense physical activity three to five days a week. Moderate is moderate, and intense is when you can talk but not sing. But let her body decide which is which.

Make sure she doesn't get overheated (and you should be a good judge of that, I hope.) Don't exercise outside when it's hot or humid. Make sure she stays hydrated.

If she's doing weights, hand her the small and medium ones.

And, just to be Captain Obvious again, here are some sports she (and you) should avoid while she's pregnant:

- weightlifting
- martial arts
- soccer
- basketball
- hockey
- baseball
- softball
- skiing
- horseback riding
- skating
- scuba diving
- wide squats or lunges

When she's working out, keep an eye on her for any of these symptoms and make her stop at once if even one manifests:

- headache
- dizziness or feeling faint
- heart palpitations
- chest pain
- swelling of the face, hands, or feet
- calf pain or swelling
- vaginal bleeding
- contractions
- deep back, pubic, or pelvic pain
- cramping in the lower abdomen
- difficulties walking
- any change in the baby's movements
- amniotic fluid leakage
- shortness of breath
- sudden fatigue
- muscle weakness

If you also stay healthy during pregnancy, this can help your partner feel strong during childbirth. Find out how you can support her during these tough times in the next chapter.

3

HOW TO SUPPORT YOUR PARTNER DURING LABOR AND DELIVERY

This chapter will provide tips on how you can support and take care of your partner during labor and delivery. If you don't intend to be in the delivery room, then you can skip this chapter unless you're just curious. But most American fathers are now present in the same room as their partners for the birth, and most American mothers-to-be want them there, too.

A brief history of delivery room dads

This wasn't always so, however. Up until the 1930s, only half of all deliveries happened in hospitals, but by the 1950s, 95 percent of American women were having their babies in the operating theatre. The fathers had to stay in the waiting room, but by the late 1940s, some had begun to take matters into their own hands. "As they wrote and read comments in 'fathers' books' that many hospitals provided as semi-public diaries," writes historian Judith Walzer Leavitt, "they took action, as one father put it, [to] grab hatchets and chop through the partition separating them from their laboring wives[1]."

It was such actions that forced the hospital authorities to allow men into the delivery room. "In the 1970s hospitals and physicians gradually relented and permitted men to be in delivery rooms, where they were positioned at the head of the table and could encourage laboring women in their work," writes Leavitt.

What people want, though, isn't necessarily best practice. However, a meta-analysis from the Cochrane Review found that "Women who received continuous labor support may be more likely to give birth 'spontaneously,' i.e. give birth vaginally with neither ventouse nor forceps nor caesarean. In addition, women may be less likely to use pain medications or to have a caesarean birth, and may be more likely to be satisfied and have shorter labors[2]."

New mothers praise new dads

The comments below aren't taken from *Amazing Stories* or *Believe It or Not* but from the pregnancy and parenting website <u>bellybelly</u>.

- "He stood there and let me squeeze the absolute crap out of his hand when I was going through contractions!" Astrolady
- "He was chatting away to the midwife about all sorts of nonsense as well, I wasn't too aware of what they were on about, but the sound of his voice was comfort enough!" JOJA
- "I couldn't have done it without him. He got me drinks (then held the sick bag for me when I vomited them back up), gave me massages, dragged me in and out of the shower, encouraged me all the time, made sure that I was always kept informed (even after the drugs kicked in) and charmed all the midwives. During the time that I was in the ante-natal ward he arrived in the morning before I woke up so I opened my eyes and there he was. He bought me food so I didn't have to eat hospital meals and looked after my cat even though he hates him." Dachlostar

- "My partner just sat by my bed and didn't say a word, which is all I wanted. Just a nice quiet room with some relaxation music playing. While in the shower he kept encouraging me and telling me I was doing great etc." Tegan
- "He was also really great during the pushing stage, he followed the midwife's lead and gave heaps of encouragement and praise, and probably contributed to it being such a short amount of pushing, because he really made me believe the end was near so I would give it my all . . ." Ambah

I wasn't in the delivery room for my daughter's birth, but I did go in for my son's. The reason we decided I shouldn't be present for my daughter was straightforward: I was more nervous about being in there than Jenny was about me not being there. However, by the time Jenny got pregnant again two years later, I was already a confident Dad, and I knew I wanted to be present when my son came into the world.

It was a strange and intense experience. Jenny was glad to have me there because she ended up having to do a cesarean. She felt calmer just being able to see me and hear my voice and hold my hand. When the doctor took out my son, he presented him to me bottom first so I could see the testicles. I was surprised at how broad his chest and shoulders were—until then, I'd always assumed newborn girls and boys looked pretty much the same.

Bottom line: it doesn't matter what the surveys and studies say about the father being present in the delivery room. (Also, ignore what your friends and relatives say.) What you decide to do depends on your partner and you and your relationship. My only advice is that you should be reasonably sure that your presence will be a calming one because giving birth is stressful enough. She doesn't need you adding to it.

And, yes, I know the main worry you have, but this is also up to you: if you think seeing your wife push a human being out of her vagina will kill your sexual attraction, either don't be in the delivery room or cover your eyes for that part like your spouse does for the gory bits in horror movies.

Before the Birth

Once you've found out that she's pregnant, you'll be having a lot of discussions about parenting, life, and the price of corn. You need to be more engaged than usual to reassure her that you're part of the whole process, even if she's the one getting bigger and bigger. Ask her questions like:

- What do you find scariest about delivering a baby?
- What stuff are you worrying about?
- What are the most important things you want to happen in the delivery room?
- What are you feeling?

Yes: "What are you feeling?" I know this last question is one you'd prefer to avoid, but this is an exception to the rule since it's your baby, too. So, ask. And pay attention when she answers, even if she's still explaining two hours later. Do active listening—i.e., repeat what she tells you in your own words so that she knows you understand what she's going through (or at least making an effort to).

Once you've both decided you'll be front and off-center, the two of you should have a detailed discussion about her birth preferences. This includes everything from whether she would prefer a natural delivery, what position she wants to be in, whether she will allow an epidural, if she wants music and scented candles in the delivery room, and whether you should start reading James Joyce's *Ulysses* when she goes into labor (so you can share her pain).

Bear in mind, though, that the old saying "Life is what happens when you're making other plans [*]" is especially applicable to the delivery room and *especially* applicable to not using an epidural. So, get to know what she wants and, just in case, make an exactly opposite list.

Just to get some knowledge (and therefore confidence), you might want to sign up for some prenatal classes with her. Here you will learn more than you ever wanted to know about labor and birth and why women are saints. Hospitals usually have these prenatal sessions or, alternatively, you can choose an independent birth education class.

Kelly Winder, founder of bellybelly, argues in favor of independent classes over hospital ones. "There is no requirement for hospital-based birth classes to adhere to any set standards," she writes. "Neither is the content required to be evidence-based, or monitored by any organization. Therefore, hospitals can do whatever they like in their own birth classes[3]."

Winder is based in Australia, but her objections are also applicable to many American hospitals, especially public ones. She offers the following nine reasons to take independent birth classes:

1. Independent birth educators are specialists in what they do.
2. The classes are not based on hospital policies but on what's best for you.
3. You'll see birth DVDs designed to inspire, not frighten.
4. Your partner will learn many more tools and options for natural pain relief and how you can help.
5. You will both find out all your options for childbirth.
6. You get what you pay for.
7. You know who you are getting.
8. You (Dad-to-be) will be more involved
9. You and your partner will get help figuring out your birth preferences (aka plan)[4].

"Many hospital-based classes focus on different drugs available, when you can be the best drug invented!" says Winder.

Now, if your partner *really* wants you in the delivery room and you *really* don't want to be there, one possible compromise is to hire a birth attendant or what the spiritual people call a doula. This is a professional birth support woman whose job is to support both the mother-to-be and you as her partner. Thus, she will prepare you for all parts of the birth plan and guide you through each stage as it's happening. More importantly, for your peace of mind, she will also be there to guide you if anything goes awry. But studies show that doulas actually help make it <u>less likely</u> that a doctor will be needed[5].

"Continuous support during labor has clinically meaningful benefits for women and infants and no known harm. All women should have support throughout labor and birth," says <u>one study</u>. "Continuous support was most effective when the provider was neither part of the hospital staff nor the woman's social network[6]."

Birth Support 101 for Dads

As you know, labor involves contractions for an average of twelve hours before the baby is born. (Yes, I know you didn't know, but try to look like you did.) These contractions help open the cervix so the baby can come out. When the cervix has been dilated to 10 centimeters, then the baby can come down the uterus to the vagina.

Being a man, you're probably wondering what tool you can get to measure the dilation. Unfortunately, none has been invented yet, which is why the finger is still the most reliable device. So, maybe the proper word is "fortunately."

In any case, you're really not there to do these tasks, which are better left up to the doctor, nurse, or midwife. You're there for moral support, which is just as important as the actual mechanics of delivery. (Refer to the list of comments above.)

Dilating on dilation

Since you probably won't be at the hospital when labor begins, it's useful to get familiar with the various stages, if only to help you keep a cool head as you get ready to go to the hospital or birth center.

Stage #1—Early Labor. Despite what you've seen in movies, this doesn't start with her water breaking and making a puddle on the floor. Instead, she will start to have mild contractions similar to her menstrual cramps, which you've surely heard about if you've been together for anything more than several months. She might also get a backache and mild diarrhea. This first stage can last from 12 to 14 hours, which means you have plenty of time to reach the hospital. Early labor is underway when her contractions are 15 to 20 minutes apart. Her cervix will dilate to about 3 cm, but you won't be measuring that.

Stage #2—Active Labor. Contractions get stronger, which can be measured by how much she's crushing your hand. In this phase, she'll probably be trying to break your metacarpals every 5 minutes for about 60 seconds at a time. By this time, you should be wherever your doctor/doula/nurse is. Tip: don't get obsessed with timing the contractions. She needs you focusing on her, not your stopwatch. Her cervix will be dilated four to seven cm but, again, you don't care.

Stage #3—Transition. This is the home stretch before baby comes. The contractions increase in strength and frequency, and the cervix dilates to 8 to 10 cm, which is a sight you may not want to behold. This is the quickest part—between 5 to 20 contractions, each 1 minute to 90 seconds long, with just 3 minutes or so between them, lasting in total anywhere from 10 to 60 minutes.

Is her body faking it?

Sometimes, the labor symptoms aren't the real thing. So, to avoid panicking and reaching the hospital too early, here's what you should look out for:

The contractions aren't (1) regular, (2) getting more frequent, (3) getting more painful, and (4) stopping if you change position or walk around.

Who are you gonna call?

So, you're timing the contractions, encouraging her, and, once the contractions start speeding up—i.e., they're getting longer, stronger, and quicker—then make your call to the doctor/midwife/doula.

Grab the birth bag for her and your go-bag with your snacks, drinks, sandwiches, and some device to pass the time.

What position does she prefer?

Take your mind out of the gutter. Especially since you won't be getting her in any positions for a few months at least. Her preferred positions for labor should be part of your birthing plan, and you're there to help her get into position (which, at least, is one thing you've had a lot of practice in.)

An upright position is best for the first stage since it helps the labor to progress, particularly with the contractions' intensity, strength, and frequency. "Upright" means standing, kneeling, sitting on a fitball, or even walking. Gravity is now her second-best friend after you, and even your position is shaky at this point. But, as with everything else, it depends on what position she finds most comfortable or convenient. If the baby decides to start coming in the wee hours, for instance, she may want to lie down just to nap.

Your job is to lie or stand with her or, if she needs it, curl yourself into a pretzel. If she's in bed, have lots of pillows handy to put under, over, or beside her—whatever she wants. Help her change positions as often as possible without being a nag.

The same positions work for the active labor stage—walking about or kneeling forward during contractions, resting between. If you mistime it and you're still at home with the contractions speeding up, get her in a doggy-style position. This takes pressure off the cervix, and here you thought it was only good for one thing. Don't let her lie on her back because that can increase her pain and can also impede (not cut off) her blood and oxygen supply because of the weight of the baby and her uterus.

6 things to look out for during labor

1. Keep an eye on her facial expressions and movements. You're probably better at reading her than anyone else in the room, so you'll know before she says anything if the pain is getting intense or if she's feeling to take a

dump. If she's licking her lips, be there with a sip of water.

2. Make sure she doesn't hold her breath.
3. Look to see if she's sweating and wipe her face and neck with a cool cloth.
4. See if her hair is getting in her face. Tie it up.
5. Watch for contractions and, when they're happening, stay quiet. Only encourage after the contraction has passed.
6. If you start to feel overly anxious, tell her you're just going out to get something and you'll be back immediately. Use that time to calm down. You don't need to be adding your stress to hers.

Tips for the final phase

- As she's screaming louder with the pain, say something along the lines of "You're nearly there, this is the shortest part, babe, you're doing great, baby's on its way."
- When the contractions are getting really bad: "Okay, babe, that was a bad one, but you're one contraction closer to our baby."
- Hold her hand and let her crush yours.
- Match deep breaths with her. Remind her to breathe every 6 to 10 seconds.
- Hold/hug her between contractions.

- Put a cool rag on her forehead or neck if she wants one.
- Have ice chips ready in a bowl or vacuum flask.
- Give her sips of water from a flask with a bendy straw.
- Help her squat if she feels more comfortable in that position.
- When the baby is out, make sure the umbilical cord doesn't get clamped right away since this is better for the baby, but the medical personnel may be more focused on wrapping up.

So now the baby's here, and your world has changed forever. Foremost on your mind is the question, "How do I take care of this little human and the big human who just pushed you out?" You'll find everything you need to know in the next chapter.

[*] According to Quote Investigator, typically attributed to John Lennon, who used the phrase in one of his post-Beatles songs, but first coined by comic strip writer Allen Saunders.

HELP OTHER NEW DADS DISCOVER THAT THEY ARE ALREADY THE QUINTESSENTIAL EXPERT ON THEIR CHILD.

"The miracle is this: The more we share, the more we have."

— LEONARD NIMOY

You might remember from the introduction that my college friend, Roger was an invaluable source of advice when I became a new dad.

A father of two kids, Roger shared an important life lesson: All I really needed to worry about was feeding, loving, and creating joyous moments with my little one.

One of the main tenets of my book is that fathers know their children like nobody else. They have their own strengths, concerns, and questions. They also have a unique insight and intuition that is sharpened through experience.

If you have more than one child, you may find that you are a lot more confident than you were as a newbie. You will have put out many fires, spent time with your baby alone, and become clued in to their needs with just a look, a sound, a cry.

However, many new dads may lack your confidence. They may feel scared that they don't know the first thing about infant care, and that they could "do the wrong thing" and somehow mess up, big time.

Seasoned fathers know that all parents make mistakes. However, parents often minimize their children's resilience. They also fail to take into account the enormous potential for growth that even small mistakes can offer us.

If this book is shedding light on how you can help your partner during pregnancy, take an active role in childcaring, or choose the best parenting style, then give other dads the chance to feel as confident as you do.

By leaving a review of this book on Amazon, you'll help someone tap into the great dad that lies within.

Simply by telling them how this book helped you and what they can expect to find inside, you'll help save them tons of research and help them get right to their many daddy duties with aplomb.

Scan the QR code for a quick review!

4

AFTER CHILDBIRTH: PROVIDING FOR YOUR BABY'S NEEDS

> *"The amazing thing about becoming a parent is that you will never again be your own first priority."*

— OLIVIA WILDE

So, baby's here, you're back home, and you have three main questions: (1) Did I really make this little creature? (2) Can I take care of this little creature? and (3) When will this little creature start looking like a little human?

This chapter provides tips on how you can support your partner after birth to take care of your newborn. And, to answer the last question first: in about two to three months. As the great comedic novelist P.G.

Wodehouse once noted, all infants look like a homicidal fried egg. As for the first question: Yes, you did, unless the DNA test says differently. (In case you're wondering, less than one percent of men aren't the fathers of the child they're raising[1], and those odds are even less for any man who's taking the time to read this book[2].)

Daddy's 3 main duties (4, if you're that kind of man)

Get baby's name right. Let's backtrack a bit to before you come home. Your first duty as Daddy is to fill out the form for the baby's birth certificate and/or make sure all the information is correct. That ensures that Ashley doesn't go through life being called Ashy. Your second duty is to make sure you have the car seat installed to protect the baby on the way home.

Stand guard. Everybody wants to come at once to see the new baby, and your job as a new dad is to tell them: "No way, José!" (Don't use that phrase if your friend is actually Mexican, though.) For one thing, you don't want your baby exposed to too many germs in their first days out in the world. For another, your wife may not want too many people around while she focuses on baby. And, last but not least, do you really want people to see the creature before it starts looking human? Because when your friends and relatives gush, "Oh, how cute!" you'll always wonder what else they've been lying about.

Don't be a boob or even two. A website named "Art of Manliness" says that men should help their wives breastfeed. The writer says, "Call me unmanly, but before Gus was born, I read a couple of books about breastfeeding, and I was very hands-on in trying to get the positioning and latching right.[3]" I'll agree to his request—you're unmanly, dude! To be sure, he says his wife appreciated the assistance but, then again, she co-wrote the article. Still, if your wife's okay with it, by all means, manipulate her boobs to get baby feeding. For us, Jenny was able to handle that most maternal of tasks, and I myself only wanted to be (man)handling her breasts for the usual reasons.

Now with that out of the way, let's get to the most important question: How do you take care of your infant baby? Your two main concerns should be (1) changing diapers and (2) not dropping the baby.

Diaper rashness

Once upon a time, men didn't change diapers. In fact, even in the 1987 movie *Three Men and a Baby*, Tom Selleck's character tells Steve Guttenberg's, "I'll give you a thousand dollars if you change her." However, according to <u>one survey</u>, between 1982 and 2000, the number of fathers who changed diapers went from 57 percent to 97 percent.[4] Now, obviously, among that 97 percent must be many men who are even dumber than you and me, so clearly you got this. In fact, I guarantee that, within days, you'll be wondering why you were so nervous about changing your newborn child.

That said, here are some hints to make your diaper change training easier. The trick is in the first fold. This is essential. So, baby is on his or her back, you pull the Velcro tabs loose, open the diaper, and immediately fold the lower (bottom) part of the diaper to enclose the poop.

That done, you raise baby's legs and cross them frog-like at the ankles, pull out the dirty diaper, and roll it up one-handed. Another technique is to rest baby's bum on the folded diaper so it doesn't open during the diaper changing process. You use a wet wipe to clean the bottom thoroughly, then open a fresh diaper, rest it under baby's bum and close all the tabs, making sure it fits securely around the thighs so no pee or poop will leak out.

Now for the bad news: that was how to change a *girl* baby. If you have a boy, matters become a little more complicated. The technique is basically the same except for that first fold. When you open the tabs of the diaper,

DO NOT—and this is crucial—fold it over the poop immediately. Instead, hold the flap up vertically for a few seconds and wait to see if he pees. If you don't do this, the pee will go right on your face and also in the poopy diaper. Then cleaning becomes a real mess. By holding the flap up, the pee will be blocked and fall back into the open diaper, which can then be folded closed.

I, for one, am thankful I had a daughter before a son because I was already a highly skilled diaper changer when baby Tyler came along. That said, I did learn the hard way about using the flap as a pee shield.

Bathing is not hard to do

Here's a brief tale of horror. When my daughter, Ashley, was less than a month old, she would only fall asleep if her mother or I was holding her and only stay asleep if we continued to do so. Once, she fell asleep on my chest as I was sitting on the sofa and, as I got up with her in my arms to go turn on the big Saturday night fight, I somehow lost my grip. I leaned backward as she slid down my forearms toward my hands, and she was literally at my fingertips before I regained my grasp. She didn't fall and didn't even wake up. But that momentary terror has remained with me since.

Moral of the story: never think about anything else while you're moving with your baby in your arms. Focus all your attention on the baby. An unexpected wriggle and you become the parent who dropped their baby on their head. Even with normal activities, and especially when you're bathing them, this is very important—which is the task we address next.

Timeline: First point: newborn babies only need bathing two or three times a week (and will still retain that baby smell, which is like breathing in life itself). You should wait about a week before giving them their first bath— not in a bathtub but with a sponge. Just don't do it right after a feeding, or else you might end up cleaning off spit-up or poop. You'll be doing sponge baths until the umbilical cord stump falls off, which usually takes about one to three weeks. You can sponge-bathe baby in a baby tub, on the bed, on the kitchen counter, or even on the floor, all on a waterproof mat.

Time of day: Should you bathe your baby in the morning or the evening? That's determined by your baby and your schedule. Babies are generally more active in the morning, so they may be less fussy about bathing then. On the other hand, an evening bath can be part of the bedtime routine, making it easier to put them to sleep. We always did bedtime baths. You do what's best for you.

Tub time: At three to four weeks after birth, you can start bathing baby in a baby tub, just like you see in all the photos. Yes, get some toys to float in the tub. Make sure the water is warm, not hot, using your elbow or wrist. For Dads who prefer exact measurements, that's not more than 120 degrees Fahrenheit (49 degrees Celsius).

Tub tips: (1) make sure you have everything you'll need laid out beforehand. You can't leave your baby in the tub, obviously, and lifting them out to go get the stuff isn't the best idea—they're already slippery from the bath, so you have to be extra careful, and they might get chilly even on the short walk to go get what you forgot. So, here's what you need:

- baby soap
- washcloths
- cotton balls
- towel
- plastic basin

If you're changing baby right there, also have a diaper at hand, diaper ointment or cream if you're using that, and baby clothes.

(2) Here's how you hold your baby for bathing. Put one arm under their head, holding her/his underarm on the

other side (so your arm is around baby), with your other arm under their bum. Slide baby feetfirst into the tub. Always keep one hand on them at all times. Always keep one hand on them at all times—yes, I repeated it. And, just in case you didn't hear me the first two times: *Always keep one hand on them at all times!*

(3) You just need about two inches of water, just covering the lower part of baby's body. You also don't want to keep them in the bath longer than the water stays warm to avoid them from getting cold. Turn on the cold water first, then adjust with the hot, and turn off the cold water last.

(4) Use a mild soap and only soap up baby's hands, bottom, and genitals (be very gentle on this last, boy or girl). Water is fine for cleaning up the rest of baby's body. For baby's face, dip the washcloth (or a cotton ball) in the warm water and wipe their eyes from the inner corner outward. Then soak the washcloth and wipe their face, especially the mouth and chin, as well as the ears (don't let water drip inside their ears, though). Then, still using the washcloth, wipe their neck, torso, under the arms, and inside all those creases of fat that are healthy on a baby and obese on an adult.

Drying off. For the final wash off, hold baby draped along your arm with the back of their head in your hand. Pour fresh warm water from a cup over their head and body. Then lay baby down on a plush towel, fold them up in it, and pat them dry. Make sure you dry their bottom and between all the creases. Then put on the diaper and clothes. That's it. Don't you feel accomplished? The nervousness will pass after the first few baths.

Bathing is more than cleanliness

You will find that bathing baby becomes a bonding experience—for you, that is, if not for baby. This isn't what you hear from most baby websites, though. For example, one such article says, "Taking care of your baby lets her know you care . . . Feeling your gentle touch and hearing your voice will let your little one know how much she's loved.[5]" This is hardly likely. While babies may like your touch and voice, they can't "know" somebody else's feelings until about two years of age. But you, as Daddy, will still enjoy that connection, and baby will become even more familiar with your presence, so by all means, go ahead.

Bathing also provides new sensory experiences for baby, and any kind of stimulation helps brain growth. The same article quoted above says, "Teach a lesson in cause-and-effect by showing how to kick the water and create a splash. And don't forget a play-by-play as you wash — name her little body parts as you bathe — and she'll be learning a tub-full of words!"

Actually, no. Babies are actually born with a sense of cause-and-effect, or what scientists call 'folk physics'.[6] So they don't learn anything from splashing water, except that it's a lot of fun getting Daddy wet. As for learning words, baby won't start understanding words till about six months[7].

Now that we've got your main concerns out of the way, let's look at the more general ways you can help take care of baby and Mommy. Here are 10 basics:

1. Give praises. Your partner is probably worrying more than you about being a good mother than you are about being a good father. Compliment her on every little baby task she gets right. Hold your tongue on what she gets wrong, or just gently suggest a different approach or method.
2. Talk about your own doubts and fears in relation to the baby. By reassuring you, she will reassure herself about how you each feel about finding your way with your new baby.
3. Share as many tasks as possible, which means basically everything except breastfeeding. And even feeding is something you'll be doing soon enough.

4. Do most, if not all, the household chores so she's less tired and has more time for baby chores. Trust me on this one.
5. Give massages, including foot massages, neck massages, and other boring body parts.
6. Put baby to sleep when you can.
7. Once she's comfortable pumping out her breast milk, you can help out by bottle feeding.
8. Let her decide when to stop breastfeeding. Many mothers have this determined by their work schedule, but some other mothers, by when baby grows teeth.
9. Don't laugh if she stops breastfeeding too soon and is groaning in pain from her engorged breasts.
10. Take turns getting up to feed baby.

Basics #10 may be the most important help you can give. As we'll discuss in the next chapter, sleep deprivation is the main problem new parents have. Since Mommy is home taking care of baby 24/7, any relief you can give her so she can get more sleep is an immense boon. At the same time, unless you have paternity leave plus vacation, you will also find it hard to feed the baby at 3 am and then head out to work from 9 to 5 or longer. In that scenario, take over the 6 pm to 9 pm feedings and, if you can manage, one more before you leave for work.

What to feed baby at what age

Breast milk and formula are the only foods your baby will need for their first four to six months. How will you know when to start solid foods? Baby will let you know, mostly by grabbing for whatever you're eating. Then you can start giving them a spoonful or three of one-ingredient foods such as pureed cauliflower, sweet potato, apple, or chicken.

By the time they're 8 to 12 months old, they should be eating a variety of soft foods. The table below lays out baby's food progression[8]:

Age	Indicators	Foods
Birth to 4 months	Rooting reflex	Breast milk or formula
4 to 6 months	Holds head upright, doubles birth weight, closes mouth around spoon.	Breast milk, formula, pureed vegetables, pureed meats, oats, barley cereal, and unsweetened yogurt.

6 to 8 months	Same as 4–6 months.	Breast milk or formula, pureed or strained fruits, pureed or strained vegetables (well-cooked carrots, squash, sweet potato), pureed or mashed meat (chicken, pork, beef), pureed or soft pasteurized cheese, cottage cheese, or unsweetened yogurt, pureed or mashed legumes (black beans, chickpeas, edamame, fava beans, black-eyed peas, lentils, kidney beans), iron-fortified cereal (oats, barley) and small pieces of bread and crackers.
8 to 12 months	Same as 6 to 8 months, also picks up objects with thumb and forefinger, transfers items from one hand to the other, moves jaw in a chewing motion, swallows food more easily, no longer pushes food out of mouth with tongue, tries to use a spoon.	Breast milk or formula, soft pasteurized cheese, cottage cheese, and unsweetened yogurt, soft-cooked vegetables (carrots, squash, potatoes, sweet potatoes), fruit mashed or cut into cubes, cereal, scrambled eggs, potato, pasta, small bits of meat, poultry, boneless fish, lentils, split peas, pintos, or black beans.

As a new dad, you will very likely find a strange gratification in feeding your baby from a bottle and, later, from a bowl. That's what mothers have from the start. That said, don't stress yourself out if your baby turns out to be a picky eater. General rule: babies know what's good for their bodies. If they don't eat what you're giving them the first time around, try again three or four days later. If they continue to reject that particular food, stop trying to make them eat it. As the table above shows, you have umpteen healthy things to offer them.

You might also want to try introducing a new food once every three or four days. Also, keep a record of what you're giving them so, in case they have an allergic reaction or just an upset tummy, you'll know what they ate over the past few days.

Some doctors recommend that you introduce new foods one at a time. If possible, wait three to five days before offering another new food. (If your baby or family has a history of allergies, talk to your baby's doctor about specific timing.) It's also a good idea to write down the foods your baby samples. If they have an adverse reaction, a food log will make it easier to pinpoint the cause.

Here's a list of <u>foods you should avoid</u> in these early stages[9]:

- honey,
- cow's milk,
- soy milk,
- fruit juice,
- sugary drinks,
- unpasteurized foods,
- foods with added sugars, and

- foods with too much sodium.

You will also want to avoid processed foods, which include many commercial baby foods. Also, make sure your baby can easily swallow everything you put in their mouth—no chunks of food, no raw vegetables, no nuts and seeds, no hard or crunchy foods, and no dollops of nut butters. If you or your family have allergies, it might be best to avoid eggs, peanuts, tree nuts, wheat, soy, fish, and shellfish until baby is a few years older.

That said, some allergies children are developing nowadays are caused by avoiding such foods entirely. Peanut allergies, for example, have risen in recent years because parents got scared by all the warnings and stopped letting their children eat peanuts at all. As a result, the children's immune systems never had a chance to develop resistance to peanuts, and now they are unable to eat nuts as a healthy snack.[10]

After baby comes Mommy

You took care of your partner before baby came along, but now you have to take care of her in a different way. The fact is, you're both in for a few rough years because you have this little human who simply cannot survive without your constant care. Since baby is more dependent on Mommy at this early stage, now is the time for you to ease her burden as much as possible. Here are some good ways to do so:

- If she's feeding baby in the wee hours, you do so during the day. Or vice versa. It's a matter of what suits her schedule, your schedule, and baby's schedule. Just make sure she isn't the one doing all the feeding once breast milk is pumped or formula is used.
- Feed your wife, too. Make her breakfast before you leave for work. Also, stock up on things like muffins, bagels, apples, cheese, almonds, granola bars, and anything she can eat easily. Cook meals to freeze, have takeout menus within easy reach from restaurants that deliver, and have microwaveable meals ready as well. If you haven't already, download every food delivery app you possibly can.
- Do whatever you can to let her get extra sleep. If your baby wakes up before her in the morning, take them out of the bedroom and into the kitchen while you're making breakfast. You can put baby in a sling carrier or in one of those clever sleepers that rock gently up and down to baby's movements. We had one, and it was a lifesaver. We used it every single day.

- When your partner is nursing, see if she needs you to bring her anything, like her phone or tablet, or do anything, like put on music or a movie for her to watch.
- Buy her little gifts, like flowers or her favorite magazine or bagels—whatever used to float her boat before the baby came along.
- Sterilize the baby's bottles and her breast pump. This is a task she has to do every day, even several times a day, and it's mundane and routine and really boring. You might be surprised how grateful she'll be if you do it. You might even get some, even if it's only what Bill Clinton didn't define as sexual relations.
- Keep track of all the baby supplies so you never run out of anything. Create a spreadsheet if you have to.

Father knows best

A few weeks in, it's likely you're already surprising yourself with how good you are at this Daddy thing. Yet, why are you surprised? It's not just because you're doing something entirely new and important. So is your partner, yet she's probably not amazed that she's coping.

Your previous doubts about yourself are unconsciously rooted in our Western culture that, since the 1960s, has increasingly ridiculed the concept of fatherhood. In the 1950s, American television portrayed fathers as dignified and responsible figures, even in comedy series such as *My Three Sons* and *Leave It to Beaver*. *The Brady Bunch* was probably the last series with a standard father figure. Now, fathers are more typically Homer Simpson and Al Bundy. Even in sitcoms based on traditional nuclear families, Tim Allen in *Home Improvement* and Ray Barone in *Everybody Loves Raymond* are mocked for their masculine attitudes.

Yet the fact is, most fathers fit none of these characters. Indeed, science contradicts popular culture. Evolutionary anthropologist Anna Machin, author of *The Life of Dad*, notes that "Fathers are so critical to the survival of our children and our species that evolution has not left their suitability for the role to chance. Like mothers, fathers have been shaped by evolution to be biologically, psychologically and behaviorally primed to parent. We can no longer say that mothering is instinctive yet fathering is learned.[11]" Be the smart, powerful, supporting, and proving father and husband your family needs you to be. Don't let anybody belittle or mock that.

Fathering is so hardwired into men's brains that, when our partners are pregnant, our testosterone levels drop (hence making it less likely we'll injure or kill ourselves doing something stupid), and our oxytocin levels rise, priming us to bond more closely with our partner and her expected offspring.

This is why you've adapted so well to being a dad. But the practical challenges are the easier part of fatherhood. In this chapter, we dealt with all of the basics except one: getting baby to sleep and, just as importantly, getting yourself and Mommy to sleep. As I noted earlier, this is the major problem new parents have, so wake up and read the following chapter about how to deal with all the sleep challenges that baby brings.

5

SLEEP TRAINING YOUR BABY

> *"I have long recommended that preparation for parenthood include a consideration of strategies for parents to cope with their own loss of sleep as well as wakeful babies."*
>
> — WILLIAM C. DEMENT, FOUNDER OF THE STANFORD UNIVERSITY SLEEP CENTER

Having a newborn baby in the home will give you a new appreciation for zombie movies, for you will spend many days (and even more nights) feeling like one of the walking dead. Did you think you had experienced the extremes of exhaustion in your former child-free life? Only if your former life was a Navy SEAL doing desert training, a mountaineer scaling Mount Everest, or an ultramarathon runner at the 50-mile marker. And even those guys probably preferred that to coping with a sleepless infant.

As comedian Tony Deyo put It: "Whoever invented the phrase 'slept like a baby,' they didn't have a baby. I don't think they'd ever even seen a baby. I think that phrase should be 'slept like an adult who doesn't have a baby."

The chart below shows how we would actually sleep if we all slept like babies.

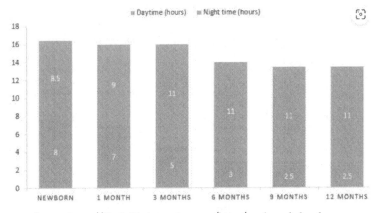

Source: https://bluebellbabymonitor.com/learn/newborn-baby-sleep.

At first glance, the ignorant nonparent might feel reassured to see that the baby sleeps from 9 to 11 hours at night. What they don't know is that those hours are interrupted every 30 minutes to 2 hours by crying to be fed, changed, cuddled, or to test Mommy's and Daddy's nerves. As a new dad, you're already painfully aware of this. But fear not: in this chapter, we will look at the importance of sleep, the benefits of sleep training, and the different methods for sleep training a baby.

Sleeping parents and other oxymorons

Sleep deprivation is a standard method of torture. Why? Because stopping somebody from sleeping creates both mental and physical distress. You can't concentrate fully, your reaction time slows, and you can't think straight. "Chronic sleep loss degrades nearly every aspect of human performance," writes medical doctor William C. Dement in his book *The Promise of Sleep*[1]. This includes loss of vigilance (ability to receive information), alertness (ability to act on information), and attention span. "In simple terms, a large sleep debt makes you stupid," Dement concludes—which means that the vast majority of parents are morons.

Dement reveals that parents of newborns lose about 2 hours of sleep every night until the baby is about 5 months old, after which they lose just 1 hour a night until the baby is a year, adding up to a grand total of 350 hours in sleep debt. That's like being awake for two weeks. Here are a few tips to get more sleep while still taking proper care of baby[2].

Sleep when baby sleeps. Since newborns nap for anywhere between two to four hours, you can grab some shuteye while they're down. Even if your sleep cycle isn't meshing with theirs, still lie down. You're more likely than not to find that you can sleep whenever baby does.

Schedule your chores around your sleep. Get in the mindset that not everything has to be done now. Understand that your home can stay untidy for a while. Your partner is more likely to be bothered by these things than you, so persuade her to let go of her OCD and do some cleaning when she's resting and you're up.

Co-sleep or put the crib near your bed. As we discussed in Chapter One, this is best practice, and it means you can soothe your baby back to sleep without getting out of bed, which in turn means you can go back to sleep more easily.

Cut out coffee. And any other beverages with high caffeine content.

Exit the Matrix. Not only can the light from screens—phones, tablets, laptops—disrupt your body's sleep cycle, but social media will probably keep you up scrolling to see what the new dance or pronoun is.

Log your baby's sleep

Our ancestors never had this problem of getting enough sleep because of their babies. This was because babies slept in the same cave or the same one-roomed hut; once the sun set, it was dark or illuminated only by flickering flames, and everybody was tired from the day's work. Most of all, the adults had no 9-to-5 schedule to keep, so they could sleep during the day if the baby kept them up. So, we can blame baby sleep challenges on capitalism.

I'm not saying that we aren't better off than our ancestors but, as far as babies are concerned, it's a whole different ball game.

Let's take a look at what you're facing:

- 0–3 months: Two-hour sleep sessions night and day. Should sleep for over 11 hours but no more than 19.
- 3–6 months: Baby will start sleeping for longer stretches at night, ranging from 4 to 6 hours. Should sleep for more than 10 hours but less than 18.
- 6 months: Most babies will sleep through most of the night.

Bear in mind that your baby may not fit this pattern. For this reason, it may be useful for you to keep a log of your baby's sleep: what times they fall asleep, for how long, what signs show that they're getting drowsy, and how long between those signs and conking out, and so on. This helps you figure out your baby's sleep cycles, which in turn allows you to plan a sleep schedule that's optimum for you. However, if they're sleeping too long or not long enough and displaying concerning signs such as lack of energy, you should check with your pediatrician.

6 ways to make sure baby (and you) sleep deep

1. *You're not getting hotter or colder.* Make sure that the room temperature is comfortable for baby. This is generally between 16 to 20°C (61 to 68°F). You can check if they're too warm by feeling whether their neck or back is clammy or sweaty. If so, either change them into something lighter or remove any blankets you might have covered them with.
2. *Soothe them with sound.* Sing or play lullabies or use white noise. The idea here is to condition your baby to associate these sounds with night and or sleep times. It's sort of like Pavlov's dogs

with possibly even more dribble. We ALWAYS use a noise machine during baby bedtime.

3. *Don't light up your baby's life.* Switch off bright lighting (fluorescent, LED) before bedtime or during night feeds and changes. Instead, install a nightlight that's bright enough for you to see but dim enough so the baby doesn't think it's daytime. Also, keep phone/tablet screens out of baby's sight at these times since the blue light might interrupt their sleep rhythm.

4. *Create a bedtime routine.* This is so important. Do the same things before you put baby to sleep. This can include a bath, feeding, and cuddling. Try to do all these around the same times and for the same length of time.

5. *Watch for signs and wonder.* When baby is drowsy, they'll start to yawn, look away, rub their eyes, and so on. You will be able to recognize these signs with ease, do not worry. Ideally, you want to put them into their cot or crib before they fall asleep. This will get them accustomed to falling asleep without you or Mommy. That, in turn, means that when they wake up during the night, they are more likely to fall back asleep without crying for you. At least, that's the theory.

6. *Bore baby back to sleep.* If they do call for you, though, don't play with baby or with your phone. Keep the lights off. Let them continue lying down, stroke them gently, and maybe sing some lullabies.

Don't rockabye baby

When baby is drowsy, you might want to put them in the crib or on the bed rather than rocking them to sleep in your arms. This is because they may come to expect rocking in order to fall asleep, which means you have to stay awake until they do. My daughter Ashley fell asleep more quickly when I rocked her than when Jenny did, so I speak from experience. I would have gotten more sleep in that first month if I had followed the put-down advice. (That said, holding her in my arms while she slept still remains one of my treasured daughter-and-daddy memories.)

It's also recommended that you teach your baby to soothe themselves—i.e., don't pick them up as soon as they start to stir or fuss, but give them some time and see if they fall back asleep on their own. This WILL be difficult but stay strong. If they learn this, they are less likely to wake you every time they wake up. Don't leave them to cry, though. When they don't fall back asleep, it's usually because they're ready to feed. At first, that will be every two to four hours but, as their stomachs expand, they'll start waking at longer intervals, every four to five hours. At six months, they usually stop needing night feeds, and then you can get a full night's rest.

Sleep as a symptom

It's important to know what the typical sleeping pattern is for babies so you can tell if your baby may be having other issues that may be affecting their sleep. Here are a few things you should look out for:

- Excessive sleepiness or insomnia. Both can be due to a growth spurt or teething, but also illness.
- Disruptive sleep apnea. This is a condition that mostly affects adults but can occasionally occur in infants, especially those who were born prematurely. It affects 84% of infants who weigh less than 2.2 pounds and 25% who weigh less than 5.5 pounds. These are the signs you should look for if you think your baby might have sleep apnea: stopping breathing for more than 20 seconds; repeated breathing pauses of less than 20 seconds; and a slow heartbeat. A

baby's heartbeat is typically between 100–150 beats per minute.

- Your baby's sleep can also be disrupted by a fever, an infection, or reflux[3].

How to train your baby

I know, I know. It sounds both ridiculous and impossible. How can anybody train any baby to do anything? And, even if we could, do we really want to? Well, it all depends on your sleep situation. Lack of sleep is inevitable once the baby comes along, but the real question is whether you're able to function in this state. If you find that sleep deprivation is affecting your life significantly, then sleep training is worth a try.

What is sleep training? Simply put, it's teaching your baby how to fall asleep without you. Here's the bad news: you can't really try it before baby is six months old, four at best. Here's the worse news: it involves deliberately letting your baby cry with no response from you (at least no immediate response).

Now, don't worry. Doing this doesn't mean your child is more likely to become a drug addict, criminal, or college dropout because Mommy and Daddy didn't love them. These days, too many parents and even grandparents seem to have forgotten that children are resilient. (But, if you need scientific support, one study concludes, "The human organism is surprisingly resilient in the face of deleterious experiences and sufficiently malleable to 'bounce back' given constructive inputs. Only the most pervasive and continuous detrimental experiences have lasting effects on development[4]."

And, according to an article on the What to Expect website, "Many experts say that sleep training is not only safe, it's healthy and important for babies' development."

As always, though, remember that no expert is as expert as you about your baby.

Let me hasten to add that sleep training doesn't mean putting your baby down in another room and letting them cry nonstop. It does mean letting them cry for a certain amount of time before you try to soothe them, so they don't expect an immediate response and that that's okay.

You can start trying the various sleep training methods when baby is between four to six months old, assuming your baby is within the typical sleep pattern—i.e., able to sleep six to eight hours during the night without a feeding. The five main approaches in this chapter are:

- Cry It Out
- The Ferber Method
- Chair Method
- Bedtime Fading Method
- Pick Up, Put Down Method

Once you've read how to use these methods, decide which one you and your partner are most comfortable (or, perhaps more accurately, least uncomfortable) with and try it out on baby. In the final analysis, it will be the baby who decides what works and what doesn't, so it's best to try all the methods unless, of course, you get really lucky and the first approach works right off the bat. (But don't hold your breath.)

Let's briefly summarize each method before getting into more detail, starting with the one least liked by nonpsychopathic parents.

Cry it out (CIO)

The <u>CIO sleep training</u> is also called the "extinction" method, which doesn't bode well for your baby. And no wonder: CIO means exactly what the acronym says— putting baby to bed and letting them cry until they fall asleep.

According to the sleep training article on What to Expect, "That means as long as you've ensured you've put your baby to bed with a full tummy and in a safe sleep environment, you won't go back into her room until it's time for her to get up the next morning or until she needs to eat next[5]."

You're supposed to do this for three to four nights. Seriously.

Their website also has a note at the end of every article stating that "The educational health content on What to Expect is reviewed by our medical review board and team of experts to be up-to-date and in line with the latest evidence-based medical information and accepted health guidelines."

Here's the thing: we didn't evolve in an environment where babies were *ever* left alone. Parents who did that were likely to have babies who got snatched up and eaten by predators, which meant that those genes went extinct. So, while I do believe babies are resilient, I also believe parents shouldn't defy the hardwired tendencies we're born with.

My nonexpert recommendation is that if you're going to try the CIO method, don't leave baby in a separate room, and don't do it for more than two nights.

Ferber method

This is a milder version of the CIO. You set a timer and let baby cry for that period. Then you increase the interval by a few minutes. Repeat until the What to Expect article says, "There's no need for these comfort check-ins because your baby has learned to self-soothe."

Yeah. We tried this with Ashley. Complete failure.

Chair method

This is sitting on a chair next to baby's crib or cot, letting them cry but not picking them up until they fall asleep. Each night, move the chair a little further away until you're in the next room.

"This method won't work for babies who can't put you out of mind until you're out of sight, however," says What to Expect.

No shit, Sherlock. And how do the article's writer and medical reviewer know what's in a baby's mind?

Bedtime fading method

For this approach, observe baby's sleep cues, such as eye rubbing, yawning, and fussing. At that point, put them to bed. If they fall asleep, voila! Mission accomplished, and you're better than Tom Cruise, who has one biological child and two ex-wives. If baby doesn't fall asleep and starts crying, pick them up for about half-an-hour. If that doesn't work, try the following night again, but move up the bedtime by about 15 minutes. Repeat until baby falls asleep almost at once.

Pick up, put down method

This means putting the baby down to sleep, waiting to see if they cry, and if they do, picking the baby up until the crying stops and putting her down again. And repeat and repeat and repeat. If she does not cry, you can leave the room with confidence.

The What to Expect writer and reviewer assure readers that "After three to four nights of methods like Ferber or cry it out, many babies are sleep trained (save a few minutes of fussing or wails before drifting off)."

Don't believe them.

In fact, they go on to say, "If you follow a sleep training method consistently and it's still not working after two weeks, you may want to call your doctor for tips and advice." Then they add, "But with time, consistency and a bit of luck, you'll soon be sleeping peacefully, and your little one will have learned the valuable life skill of how to fall and stay asleep all on her own."

Falling asleep is a life skill? Okay, then.

I'm not saying not to try these methods. I'm saying that use them without expecting easy results. It takes time, patience, and readiness for failure. But, yes, if any of the methods work, even partially, this will be an immense help for you and your partner.

Take account of the <u>following caveats</u> [*]:

- Some babies fall asleep easily (apparently, they acquire this "life skill" after one month with no training) and have a sleep pattern that allows both themselves and Mommy and Daddy to get enough rest. Other infants are more wakeful and will need more nurturing and training to sleep in a way that helps the parents get on with normal life.
- All babies are different, and that is so even for babies within the same family. Ashley was a wakeful baby. Tyler slept like a baby-less adult from the time he was one month old. So, even if one sleep training method worked for the first child, there's no guarantee it will work for the second.

- If no method works, forget the experts, and do what your intuition says is best. Say it again with me: "You are more expert about your child than any expert."
- Both babies and grown-ups wake up several times during the night. So, even if you successfully sleep train your baby, that doesn't mean continuous nights of baby-free bliss. In any case, <u>sleep regression</u> may well occur, and you might even have to do some more rounds of sleep training[6].

In the next section, we look at each of the sleep training methods listed above in (excruciating) detail.

Crying It Out

Here are the <u>basic steps for CIO</u>:

- *Step #1.* Look for baby's sleepy signs—rubbing eyes, yawning, crankiness, etc.
- *Step #2.* Begin baby's bedtime routine—bath, feeding, lullabies, reading, massage, or what have you.
- *Step #3.* Put baby in crib/cot/bassinet while still awake.

- *Step #4.* Leave the room without waiting for baby to fall asleep.
- *Step #5.* Let baby cry until they fall asleep.

Let's talk a bit about Step #5. This is the main goal of CIO—to let baby cry until he or she wears themselves out and falls asleep. According to the What to Expect experts, this may take about 45 minutes to an hour. "Most parents who try the cry it out method find their babies cry increasingly less over the first three nights and their crying virtually ends somewhere between the fourth and seventh nights," says the article (which, paradoxically, also says that parents should try CIO for two weeks. "Eventually babies may simply fuss or screech in complaint for a couple of minutes — or simply quietly fall asleep[7]."

If that happens with your baby—assuming you have the guts to try this approach—all well and good. If not, feel free to send a stern letter to Heidi Markoff. In fact, even the article's authors, after writing that this method will work within days, then say, "Cry it out isn't for everyone, and it doesn't work for every baby. And that's perfectly okay." Talk about talking out of both sides of your mouth!

By the way, they also warn that baby may vomit during CIO training with all the crying. And, once your pediatrician has confirmed that there's no health issue, "the vomiting usually stops after a few nights at most." We never tried this method. I refuse to believe that letting your baby cry relentlessly without trying to help them is somehow ok.

The Ferber Method

This approach, named after pediatrician Richard Ferber who developed it in the 1970s, is based on the premise that falling back asleep is not automatic but a skill that has to be learned. It's a less extreme version of CIO since, although parents still leave their babies to cry, they check on them at regular intervals. These check-ins are gradually extended until baby starts falling asleep on their own.

"Ferber's method seems to help infants make the transition from consolidated sleep with the least amount of stress for both child and parent," writes Dr. Dement. "The typical 'Ferberization' takes only two or three nights[8]."

(Dement was a mentor of Ferber, and Ferber acknowledged Dement's encouragement in his book *Solve Your Child's Sleep Problems*.)

Here's how you do the Ferber method:

- Once baby starts showing signs of sleepiness, do the bedtime routine, then put baby into the crib/cot/bassinet while they're still awake.
- Leave the room.
- When the crying starts, don't go at once. Instead, wait for a set time (see schedule below). Once the interval has passed, go back in the room, soothe your baby by patting or singing, but don't pick them up or feed them.
- Repeat as needed.

This is Dr. Ferber's recommended schedule (which is seven nights, not the two or three Dr. Dement says are typical).

Day 1

- First check-in after: 3 minutes
- Second check-in after: 5 minutes
- Third check-in after: 10 minutes
- Subsequent check-in after: 10 minutes

Day 2

- First check-in after: 5 minutes
- Second check-in after: 10 minutes
- Third check-in after: 12 minutes
- Subsequent check-in after: 12 minutes

Day 3

- First check-in after: 10 minutes
- Second check-in after: 12 minutes
- Third check-in after: 15 minutes
- Subsequent check-in after: 15 minutes

Day 4

- First check-in after: 12 minutes
- Second check-in after: 15 minutes
- Third check-in after: 17 minutes
- Subsequent check-in after: 17 minutes

Day 5

- First check-in after: 15 minutes
- Second check-in after: 17 minutes
- Third check-in after: 20 minutes
- Subsequent check-in after: 20 minutes

Day 6

- First check-in after: 17 minutes
- Second check-in after: 20 minutes
- Third check-in after: 25 minutes
- Subsequent check-in after: 25 minutes

Day 7

- First check-in after: 20 minutes
- Second check-in after: 25 minutes
- Third check-in after: 30 minutes
- Subsequent check-in after: 30 minutes[9]

You can find the chart below or online to print it out.

Progressive Waiting: The Schedule

Day	Schedule
1	3 min (1st wait), 5 min (2nd wait), 10 min (3rd wait), 10 min (subsequent waits)
2	5 min, 10 min, 12 min (subsequent waits)
3	10 min, 12 min, 15 min, 15 min (subsequent waits)
4	12 min, 15 min, 17 min, 17 min (subsequent waits)
5	15 min, 17 min, 20 min, 20 min (subsequent waits)
6	17 min, 20 min, 25 min, 25 min (subsequent waits)
7	20 min, 25 min, 30 min, 30 min (subsequent waits)

aka "Cry It Out", method by Dr. Richard Ferber

As with the CIO, there are certain strategies you can use to increase your chances of success with the Ferber method. Here are a few tips:

- *Start at the right time.* Don't start sleep training if baby is teething, ill, or even out of sorts. You also want to start during a period when there will be no disruptions, such as you heading back out to work after paternity leave or the new babysitter starting.

- *Try to stop, if at least reduce, nighttime feedings.* This is because feeding can disrupt baby falling asleep and self-soothing when they wake up during the night. Also, feed at the start of the bedtime routine rather than near the end.
- *Stop letting your baby sleep or nap anywhere but in the crib/cot/bassinet.* You want to strengthen the association between sleep and a specific location.
- *Both you and your partner should figure out how to do it.* Babies often associate Daddies with play rather than rest. This might make it easier for your partner to sleep train baby. Be aware of this so you can both decide what role each of you plays in this process.
- *Consistency is key.* As with CIO, it will be difficult, even for a specific interval. But push through for the three days at least, and the full seven if you see signs of progress.

That said, if baby still isn't falling asleep by the end of a week (maybe two), take a break. You can try again with the Ferber method if you like or use one of the other approaches. (Do not use "cry it out" - it is unlikely to work if Ferber failed.)

Chair method

This basically involves sneaking away from your baby. You put the chair close to the crib and wait for them to sleep, moving the chair further away with each session until they fall fast asleep while you're in the next room with a glass of wine toasting, "Chairs."

Here are the steps:

1. Standard nighttime routine.
2. Cue sleep cues. Put baby in the crib while still awake but drowsy.
3. Sit next to her crib till baby falls asleep. You can sing a lullaby or talk nonsense.
4. If your baby wakes up after falling asleep, repeat (c). But don't pick the baby up.
5. On the third night, move the chair halfway between the crib and door and do (c) from this spot.
6. Repeat (e) from a further distance, but with less lullabies or babbling or shushing.
7. From the hall or adjoining room, listen to hear if baby wakes up. If that happens, don't reenter the room but let baby know you're close by.

As you can tell, this approach[10] takes a lot longer. But it's also less stressful for you and for your baby than CIO and Ferber.

Pick up and Put Down[11]

This approach will probably find favor with most parents. The only caveat is that it takes a lot more effort, as the name implies.

Here are the steps:

- Bedtime routine.
- Put baby in bed when sleepy but awake.
- Shush them and leave the room without lingering, sending the message to baby that all is well.
- Wait outside the door and listen.
- If baby starts crying or fussing, then wait one minute before going in to comfort them by picking them up.
- When they've calmed down (and before they fall back asleep), put them back in their crib and again leave without lingering or looking back.
- Repeat 4 and 5.

For the second night of Pick Up, Put Down, you do everything the same, except you now wait three minutes for step 5.

On the third night, same thing but now five minutes. And so you go, adding two minutes every night so your baby learns to self-soothe and fall back asleep without you. This might take a few weeks, though.

Tired nature restored

Whatever strategy you come up with, it's important that you, as a parent and especially as a dad, get back to your normal sleeping habits as soon as possible. You are the one more likely to get into an accident or make mistakes at work because of lack of sleep. And, for baby, proper sleep is also crucial for brain development.

Aside from their physical well-being, your baby also needs to develop mentally and emotionally. This can also be done by bonding with them. The next chapter will help you do this.

[*] These cautions are from the same writer of the gung-ho sleep training article in What to Expect, but with a different medical reviewer. See what I mean about dismissing the experts?

6

BONDING WITH YOUR BABY: HELPING THEM DEVELOP THEIR MENTAL AND EMOTIONAL HEALTH

I f you're anything like me, you were surprised how your world shifted the first time you saw your newborn child. "Shocked" might be the better word. For me, in virtually an instant, my priorities were reordered, my sense of self changed, and my understanding of love itself was transformed. Sure, we love our parents, our siblings, our friends, and our spouses. But absolute and unconditional love is reserved for our small children. (Sorry, animal lovers, pets don't count.)

What surprised me, too, was my own surprise. Everybody takes it for granted that mothers automatically bond with their babies. After all, they carried the child inside their own bodies for nine months and, when they're born, feed them from their own bodies for another four months to a year. But how do fathers bond with baby?

Well, let's get a few things out of the way. First of all, mothers don't actually bond with their baby at once. For most women, it actually takes about two weeks before they truly begin to feel that maternal closeness. This is probably a psychological mechanism developed from our ancestral days when the high infant mortality rate made it unwise for mothers to immediately form an attachment—in fact, in many cultures, it is considered unlucky to name a baby until two weeks have passed.

Second, responsible fathers feel a bond with their children from the moment they are born because the male protective instinct kicks in as soon as we hear that first crying breath and see this frail and defenseless little creature. Fathers who take care of their babies regularly have elevated levels of a hormone called prolactin, which is the same hormone involved in mothers producing breast milk.

Just as importantly, the bond is reciprocated. Little girls love their daddies, even when the daddies aren't good fathers. Sons are not so forgiving but, when a father is caring and committed, the father-son bond is a unique relationship. "Babies are born to bond," writes journalist Christine Gross-Loh. "Babies learn to empathize with others through their utter connectedness to us... babies imitate us. They respond with distress to the cries of other infants. They become distressed when our own faces are blank and unmoving[1]."

Third—and this is what you don't hear much about— the father-child bond helps children develop better than they otherwise might. "Children whose fathers played with them, read to them, took them on outings, and helped care for them had fewer behavioral problems in the early school years, and less likelihood of delinquency or criminal behavior as adolescents," writes journalist Paul Raeburn in *Do Fathers Matter?*

This chapter will examine the importance of bonding with your baby to help them develop their mental and emotional well-being and manage their emotions.

Let's begin by examining your baby's psychology.

I got you, baby

As you know by now, newborn babies have only five activities in life: sleep, cry, feed, poop, and cry some more. Same with feelings—they only have five: hunger, pain, fear, pleasure, and more hunger.

It might be more accurate to call these reflexes, though. And, within a month, you'll be seeing (or thinking you see) your baby expressing at least some of the <u>eight primary in-built emotions</u>:

1. Anger
2. Sadness
3. Fear
4. Joy
5. Interest
6. Surprise
7. Disgust
8. Shame

All <u>these emotions</u> are mediated by personal interactions, social norms, and cultural contexts. Shame, for example, is a feeling that your child probably won't express until they're about five or six years old, and how they express it depends on whether they're American or Japanese, as well as what they find shameful. Our secondary emotions are variations of these eight primary ones—e.g., resentment is usually based on anger, anxiety is a type of fear, and pleasure is a form of joy.

Children get their emotional cues from their parents and other people around them, but since parents are usually the main caregivers, these are their primary models. (Later on—and much sooner than you think—their older peers will become their models for appropriate behavior.) Your role as Dad is to expose your kids to emotional cues that, typically, their mom won't. Dads help their children to manage their emotions, especially stress.

As a new father, you're not dealing with any complex emotions from baby. However, it's useful to understand the developmental stages so you can lay the foundation for your future bonding from now[2].

Infants: Babies are born with specific reflexes, instincts, and emotions. The sucking reflex, for example, ensures that they start feeding once a nipple finds their mouths. They instinctively like being cuddled. And they feel distress and pleasure. Thus, they cry to avoid unpleasant sensations (like hunger) and coo or gurgle when being rocked.

There is some evidence that, in their first six months, infants can soothe themselves through behaviors such as sucking. This is why pacifiers work. Toddlers, according to other studies, can also develop self-regulation skills in infancy, which let them decide on their own accord whether to engage or avoid certain challenges.

Toddlers: By the time they're one year old, children begin associating their parents (or other main caregivers) with their own emotional state, pleasant or distressed. Some studies find that fear is the most difficult emotion for toddlers to handle. Fathers are especially good at helping their children learn to <u>deal with fear</u> [3], often through what's called rough-and-tumble play—e.g., throwing children up in the air, which fathers do more than mothers.

By the time they're two years old, most children start to regulate their own emotions, albeit by just avoiding things that upset them and doing things they like (and demanding that Mommy and Daddy do them—often the latter because, as Raeburn points out, "infants actually preferred to be held by their fathers—because fathers were likely to play with them, while mothers were likely to feed them or change their diapers."

Childhood: As they get older, children learn what is appropriate and inappropriate emotional expression (e.g., hitting vs. hugging). How well they express themselves depends on a psychological trait called extraversion (not extroversion) that is largely genetic in nature. But many children still have difficulty conveying what they're feeling, especially if they haven't learned to name their emotions. Since men tend to have this issue no matter what their age, warm fathers accelerate the process of emotional development in their kids. Raeburn notes that "Fathers have a particularly strong influence on children's social development.

Interactions between fathers and their sons and daughters that are playful, affectionate, and engaging predict later popularity in school and among peers, perhaps by teaching children to read emotional expressions on their fathers faces, and later on those of their peer group."

The name is bond, Daddy bond

As I mentioned in the Introduction, research on fathers only really started about fifteen to twenty years ago. So, there are reams of data on mother-infant bonding, but scientists still don't know that much about the family as a whole because most of their observations and experiments treated the father as irrelevant.

However, the father research that does exist suggests that involved fathers correlate with <u>positive outcomes</u> for children. This was actually known for many decades by default: children from <u>homes with absent fathers</u> were more likely to do poorly in school, drink or take drugs, become pregnant, and commit crimes. There is correlation between early father-infant bonds and the happiness of the entire family. By contrast, children who grow up in stable two-parent families where the father is an involved parent reap a number of benefits. These include:

- Boosts in physical and mental development
- Less likelihood of depression as teens and adults
- Boys learn to handle stress better
- Academic success
- Better health[4]

That said, none of these studies take the effects of genes into account. So, if it is that fathers with higher IQs tend to be more involved with their kids, then academic success is explained by the children having high IQs rather than the father's involvement. In other words, IQ is causal and involvement correlational. Similarly, conscientiousness is a trait that is genetically influenced, which may explain both father involvement and taking better care of one's health.

However, when it comes to personal interactions, genes only account for 30 percent of behavior, while the home environment accounts for 36 percent (the remaining 34 percent is influenced by peers, social norms, other adults, and personal experiences[5].) That means that parents, and fathers in particular, can have a significant bonding experience with their children.

Let's be clear, though: when baby is small, meaning less than one year old, most of this bonding is one way. Babies don't yet have the cognitive capacity to bond with you in any meaningful way (which is not to say that emotional bonding won't happen at some instinctive level).

The key here is to be around baby as much as possible. These 12 strategies let you do this as part of your normal father-husband routine:

1. *Get a sling.* This lets you keep baby with you while you're going for a walk or doing chores around the house.
2. *Change diapers.* What's a more powerful bonding experience than wiping another human being's butt? Except for watching *Die Hard* together.
3. *Bottle feed.* This lets baby see you as not the mommy who's nonetheless doing what Mommy does. Just as Mommy cuddles baby close and looks into their eyes during feeding time, you can do the same, except you should make funny faces because that's the kind of thing Daddies do.
4. *Horsey rides.* And other things Mommy can't or won't do.
5. *Stop crying.* That is, stop baby crying. If you're crying, you need to cut down on the estrogen. When you comfort baby, you set the foundation

for later closeness, when they will turn to Daddy to make it all better.

6. *Have a dance party*. Hold baby in your arms and play that funky music. (Or dancehall or K-pop or Bollywood songs, whatever turns your crank, dude.) Baby will more likely than not prefer the faster dances—just make sure to hold the back of their neck.

7. *Dr. Daddy*. See about them when they have a cold or fever or just feel out of sorts. If their nose is stuffy, a definite Daddy duty is sucking the snot out. You can use the snot sucker thingamajig, but real men need nothing but lips and suction.

8. *Put baby to bed*. This is definitely a bonding routine, but beware: you may end up, like I did, telling *Little Red Riding Hood* every night for three months straight[6].

9. *Bathe with baby*. Generally. Babies like getting clean and, hopefully, so do you. Also, the skin-to-skin contact releases oxytocin, a stress-reducing hormone. Bathing in the bathtub allows for more play, but showers are good, too.

10. *Daddy's home*. It's good to make this a <u>bit of a ritual</u> [7], especially if you work long hours. Use a set phrase like "Daddy's back," and hug your son or daughter. Do some specific activity with

them, too, like playing with their favorite toy with them for a little while.

11. *Book bonding.* The great advantage of reading to your child before they can even understand words is that you can read what interests you. Appreciate this now, before you have to read *Green Eggs and Ham* over and over again. The important thing is not what you read but how you read it. Reading to baby gets them familiar with your voice, your smell, and your touch. They won't remember any of it, but these sensations may well remain embedded in some primitive part of their rapidly growing brains. Also, having a father who reads means they will easily pick up this skill when school time starts.

12. *Baby steps.* You will soon discover that lifting baby is a workout routine in itself. Unless you were a weightlifter before, your arms would never be stronger. Mommies carry babies around more easily because they can rest them on their hips. Men have to use their upper body strength and, while babies aren't heavy, they feel so after you've been carrying them for a while. This is why walking about with baby and, later, cycling with them or using a jogging stroller helps you keep fit while bonding over sweat.

Do play around

Here's one of the most fundamental principles of child development: play is children's work. It is through play that children learn pretty much all the skills they will need when they grow up: physical control, emotional expression, and social interaction. And, because Daddies play with children more than Mommies, this is where you shine with baby.

One study says, "Fathers may play specific and important roles, with men in some cultures having clearly defined roles as playmates to their children. Third, paternal play styles predict later socio-emotional development while paternal involvement seems to predict adult adjustment better than maternal involvement does[8]."

Play is important for children's mental and emotional growth. It helps them:

- feel loved
- develop confidence
- build relationships with other kids (and Daddy)
- develop their social and language skills

"Research suggests that play is also critical for emotional health, possibly because it helps kids work through anxiety and stress," says Scientific American. And, of particular interest to Dads, "Play fighting also improves problem solving[9]."

In playing with your child, you should divide playtime into goal-oriented tasks that you set and follow your child's lead. Don't interfere too much—offer to help but don't make it an order or wait until your child asks for help. And, if you see them doing something a bit risky, don't run to stop them at once. A few bruises may lead to tears in the short term but, in the long, such incidents help build our child's confidence and ability to calibrate risk.

You can also use play to help your child express their emotions. Puppet play, singing songs and nursery rhymes, and messy play are especially useful for this.

Last but not least, find ways, if possible, for you and your child to play outside in natural settings and parks. This lets them explore the natural environment, which is both stimulating and calming. Germany, Denmark, and Sweden actually have "forest kindergartens" for exactly this purpose. One study found that "children's academic attainment, social development, and emotional well-being increased as a result of Forest School, and did well in comparison to peers who didn't participate, whole school and national data[10]." The study also showed that playful social interactions in

Forest School support emotional resilience that fed into academic attainment. Open space play is also useful for inculcating a sense of freedom and wonder.

"Men seem to have a tendency to excite, surprise, and momentarily destabilize children," writes child psychologist Daniel Paquette. "They also tend to encourage children to take risks, while at the same time ensuring the latter's safety and security, thus permitting children to learn to be braver in unfamiliar situations, as well as to stand up for themselves."

Balancing baby and everything else

The last point, about working long hours, is a challenge many new dads face. In fact, research shows that men tend to work harder after they become fathers, probably because they're now even more highly motivated to protect and provide. But you might lose your relationship with your children by working so much you hardly see them. So you need to consciously strive for work-life balance now in a way you might not have done before baby came along. Here are some tips for doing so:

1. *Decide what your goals are.* Some of your goals will be short term, some long term. For your short-term goals, set a daily, weekly, or monthly schedule. Make sure it's a schedule that includes things you like to do and that you can manage, logistically speaking. Baby will be part of this schedule. For your long-term goals, decide what success looks like to you. Do you want to work on weekends or play hoops with your son? How do you get ahead professionally while making sure the children are happy when Daddy comes home? "It's really a misconception that you can juggle work and family," says Alan Kearns, career coach and founder of CareerJoy. "You'll find that it's easy to not meet the expectations of your partner and your firm. Finding that balance takes practice and failure before you can eventually master that fine art[11]."

2. *Plan your time with your partner.* Yes, it's unromantic. (More on this in Chapter Seven.) But it will be almost impossible for you to find sufficient time for work and family without her help. Start by estimating how much time with baby you need, block out hours for this, and then you and her map out a general schedule that works for both of you.

3. *Create more hours in your day.* How? Easy. Get off social media. If you can't do it completely, set time limits for yourself. Most people <u>spend about 147 minutes a day</u> between all the social media platforms they use. That's about seven years of your life[12]. Use the extra hours to be more productive *and* spend time with baby.

4. *Make the pandemic policy that didn't work for you.* Did you work from home during the pandemic because of lockdowns? If so (and if your work didn't suffer), then you can make a case to your company to let you work from home for at least a few days. Another alternative is to ask for flextime, which at the very least, should reduce the hours you're stuck in traffic.

And always follow the basics of self-care:

- Don't eat too much and exercise the right amount.
- Get enough <u>rest.</u>
- Make time for challenging activities you enjoy (i.e., not watching TikTok videos, though you can make some)
- Keeping up with old friends or making new ones
- Managing stress, anxiety, and anger

When bonds break

While most babies are easy to bond with (once you put in the time and effort), a minority of children tend to have behavioral issues that make bonding more difficult. *This does not mean that anything is psychologically wrong with the child!* In researching this chapter, I came across some appalling articles that insisted on framing children's behavior as "mental health" issues[13]. Children do *not* have poor mental health. They may have genetic predilections for conditions such as schizophrenia or depression, but those don't really manifest until they're in their 20s or 30s.

That said, certain behavioral issues may disrupt all your efforts at bonding. These include:

- inconsolable crying
- resistance to soothing
- avoiding eye contact
- withdrawal
- not sleeping or eating well over a long period
- very clingy
- losing skills, such as previously acquired vocabulary
- extreme tantrums on a regular basis
- having unexplained or sudden changes in behavior

Many of these signs could indicate autism, which is not a psychological condition but a mental disability. At any rate, if you're worried about your child's behavior, you should seek professional help. Some options are:

- your GP
- your child and family health nurse
- your pediatrician
- your local community health center
- mental health services
- parent helplines

Bonding with babe

Bonding with your baby will engage you fully, but you shouldn't let it. After all, your partner needs care and affection, too, and may well be feeling ignored. The next chapter looks at how you can negotiate the many challenges, tripwires, and stresses that a baby puts on a relationship.

KEEPING YOUR ROMANTIC RELATIONSHIP STRONG

I've mentioned several times that the greatest surprise about having a baby is how completely they change your view on life. Here's the second greatest surprise: a baby can make your relationship with your spouse worse.

This shocks couples because, naturally, we expect the opposite effect. After all, the two of us have brought a new person into the world. What other act could draw two people closer together? In fact, when the first study on this phenomenon was done in 1957, psychologists themselves were skeptical[1]. Unfortunately, subsequent investigations in the 1970s and 1980s confirmed the fact: the practical effects on a couple's romantic relationship when baby comes can be dire.

I knew this even before I read the studies from personal experience. Joyful as Jenny and I were at the arrival of Ashley, we did get on each other's nerves pretty much every day for those first few months. We handled Tyler's second coming a lot better, but that was because we now knew what to expect and had put in the work to make sure our relationship wasn't disrupted like before.

Here's the good news: even though babies reduce marital satisfaction, couples who don't have children are more likely to get divorced than couples with children. (Yes, I know that isn't good news for childless couples, but they're not likely to be reading this book, are they?) This chapter will discuss the issues you may encounter in your relationship after having a baby and how to address them to keep your relationship strong.

It may not be easy at first but, with love and respect and patience, you can definitely make it. That said, keeping the flame alive in your marriage after baby does take a deliberate effort, especially on the man's end.

Why does the main responsibility fall on you? Because that's just how it is, dude—man up and deal with it. But, if you really want to know, here's what the psychologists who study marital relationships have discovered.

One study found that "as couples become parents, there is a dramatic decrease in positive marital interchanges, a dramatic increase in marital conflict, and a precipitous decline in marital satisfaction. These findings were particularly pronounced for wives and in some cases were found only for the wives; however, the wife's declining marital satisfaction is a lead indicator of the husband's later declining marital satisfaction[2]."

In other words, as a contented man, you may not even be aware that your partner is unhappy with your relationship. So, you need to anticipate and take action. Interestingly, the same study I just cited found factors that helped a couple weather the challenges that came with baby. "The more fondness for his wife the husband expresses, or the more glue he puts into the relationship, the more satisfied the wife is with the marriage over the transition to parenthood," said the researchers.

So, if you're an expectant dad, make sure you express your love for your wife and do everything you can to demonstrate that love. (In other words, follow all the good advice I've given you over the past six chapters.) If baby is already here, the rest of this chapter will show you what you can begin doing to overcome these post-baby challenges to your relationship.

Geneticist and author John Medina in his book *Brain Rules for Baby* identifies four main sources of conflict for couples after having a baby: (1) sleep loss, (2) social isolation, (3) unequal workload, and (4) depression[3]. We dealt with helping your partner in Chapter Four and tackled sleeping issues in Chapter Five. So, in this chapter, we'll be focusing mainly on how to deal with other challenges to your romantic relationship (except depression, which is a clinical issue that requires professional intervention).

Let's start by looking at seven common problems:

1. *Doing the dishes.* And the laundry and vacuuming and making the bed and so on and so on. Famed clinical psychologist Jordan Peterson explains why it's important for couples to pay attention to chores as the basis for a strong romantic relationship, even though such details may seem trivial. "Your life is mostly composed of what is repeated routinely," he writes. "You either negotiate responsibility for every single one of these duties or you play push and pull forever, while you battle it out nonverbally, with stubbornness, silence, and half-hearted attempts at cooperation. That is not going to do your romantic situation any good[4]."

But, even if you and your partner have reached a working accommodation on all these tasks, baby destroys that détente. For one thing, a new mommy doesn't have as much time or energy to do what she normally does, which is probably the lion's share of the housework. For another, baby brings in a new set of chores, from changing diapers to sterilizing bottles, that didn't exist before. In the absence of a detailed plan beforehand or a clear schedule afterward, you and your partner can end up quarreling over a dirty saucer.

One solution is to sit down together and list all the tasks that need to be done, then decide how to divvy them up. Depending on each of your preferences, you may decide to switch every week or go 50-50. If that works for you both, fine. My advice, though, is that tasks should be allocated according to what each person prefers (or hates least). You also allocate according to who is better at what, but be cautious with that metric: the man may think he's good at a particular task, but the woman disagrees (and, yes, it's always the woman who's not satisfied with how the man folds the clothes).

It's also useful to express your appreciation for what your partner does. That includes having your baby.

2. My parenting is better than your parenting. Ideally, this is something you should discuss before baby comes. But, unless you and your partner are active adherents of different faiths, parenting preferences are not typically something people discuss until baby is there on the bed, crying instead of sleeping. Then the differences jump out.

"Let him cry for a bit so he doesn't get spoiled," says Mommy.

"No, pick him up at once so he doesn't get insecure and can't ask a girl out and stays single and you never have grandchildren," says Daddy.

"I'll give him the pacifier," she says.

"Do you want him to get buck teeth? Then no girl will like him, and you'll never have grandchildren unless we spend $5,000 in braces," says Daddy.

And so on.

Here are two facts: first, neither you nor your partner knows which parenting strategy is more effective; and, two, no matter what you do or don't do, your child is more likely than not to turn out fine.

That said, you should each adopt each other's suggestions and see what, in practical terms, works out best. See this as both of you learning from each other about what's best for your child—a cooperative adventure rather than a competition.

3. Less or no sex. Schedule sex: when and, depending on your situation, for how long. This might sound unromantic, but that's only because it is. You have to think of it this way: what's more romantic—planned sex or no sex at all? (See the final section in this chapter on reviving your sex life.)

4. *And baby makes three—all the time.* "After the birth of a child, couples have only about one-third as much time alone together as they had when they were childless," writes Medina. "The thrill of having a child wears off, but the incessant job of parenting does not. Being a mom or dad then becomes a duty, then a chore."

Whether you realized it or not, it took you a fair amount of time to work out relating to each other one-on-one. Apart from the relationship dynamics, you and your partner had achieved a certain understanding of living and being together in terms of conversation, activities, and daily routines.

Now, all that's gone. The addition of the third little human means that you now have to relate to your partner and baby, and she has to do likewise. This basically means starting your relationship over from scratch. No longer are you Bob the Boyfriend and she Gidget the Girlfriend, but you're now also the dad and she the mom, and both of you the caregivers.

As with sex, scheduling helps negotiate the bumps that come with these new roles and new interactions. Apart from dates (very important!), you should even set aside times to talk about household and baby-care matters, whether it's deciding on laundry day for that week or checking out preschools. That way, the rest of the time can be more me-you time, even though baby's right there looking at you as though all your attention should be on their cute self.

5. No me time. You also need to set aside time to be alone and, by "you," I mean her. Okay, you can get time to go to the gym or play Call of Duty or go for a bike ride. But that's it. Maybe you can meet with your buddies for a drink, but not for several hours, and maybe it's still not the best idea if they're all childless or, worse, single.

6. Grandparents and other pests. If your partner's parents or yours live fairly close to you, then you'll probably be seeing them a lot. Maybe even more than you've done since you were a teenager. After all, baby binds two families together and, for grandparents, grandchildren give all the upsides of parenting and none of the downs. Now, this can be a lifesaver when you need free babysitting. But, if you or your partner find that they're too intrusive and disrupting your lives as new parents, you have to set some boundaries. Set specific times when they can visit and give them regular updates on how baby is doing (don't forget to send a video). That should establish a balance that works for both you and them.

7. You can't rob a bank. Babies don't need to be hugely expensive, but couples do tend to feel a financial strain after they come along. It's not only the additional expenses—you knew you would have to buy diapers; you just didn't know how much poop a small baby can produce daily—it's also that one of you will want to stay home and see about the baby all day. And that one is most likely not you.

Gayle Peterson, Ph.D., a family therapist in Berkeley, California, and author of *Making Healthy Families*, says, "People believe they don't have enough money to raise a family, and they just freak out. You're not going to take out your anxiety about money on your baby, so you lash out at your spouse[5]."

Peterson suggests that couples talk honestly about what each of them wants now that they're a family.

"Often there's a spouse who really wants to stay home for a year instead of working, but is afraid of the cost. But there are a lot of solutions to financial problems," she says.

If baby hasn't come yet, you can try living on one salary while saving the other, so you have a financial cushion for after the birth. You can also draw up a list of needs and wants and, even with the needs, find cheaper substitutes. If you're still struggling, it may be worth your while, literally, to go to a financial consultant.

No money, no honey

I want to go into a bit more detail on the finance issue. We're brought up to believe that love conquers all, but you can't buy groceries by gazing into each other's eyes. Baby puts enough strain on a relationship without adding financial woes as well. Here are a few tips to ease the burden:

- *Cut down on luxuries.* If you order out five times a week, cut it down to three or less. Cook more. If the time it takes to cook means more hassle with baby duties, use frozen foods like pizza as a shortcut. You can also download some apps to keep track of your spending.
- *Have money for emergencies.* Repairs to your vehicle or home can disrupt your monthly budget, especially if you have to use your credit cards to pay for them. So, preferably before baby comes, you should try to have money squared away specifically for unexpected expenses. The same holds for holiday expenditures, from Christmas to Thanksgiving,

along with special events like weddings and birthdays.

- *Shop at thrift stores.* You'll find things for both you and baby, from clothing to accessories.
- *Cancel subscriptions.* You probably signed up for a lot of things during the pandemic lockdowns that you don't need now. Check your credit cards and act accordingly.

Good housekeeping[6]

I also want to delve more deeply into the <u>chores issue</u> since, as Jordan Peterson points out, getting this right helps ensure you get most other issues right, too.

Log on. Keep a log of all your chores/activities for the week with home and baby, and ask your partner to do the same.

You can print the chart at the URL below from the website What Were We Thinking!

WWWT Worksheets/Strategies: Parent's workload with a new baby (whatwerewethinking.org.au)

When you sit down with your lists at the end of the week, discuss the following questions:

- How efficient are you at each task on a scale of 1 to 5?
- Is there anything on your list you want to exchange with your spouse?
- Is there any task you really hate doing?

Make sure you simply state your preferences or dislikes without casting blame on your partner (very easy to do inadvertently) or presenting yourself as a saint (you're probably not).

Also, don't drop hints when you feel overwhelmed and want help. Or, rather, tell your partner not to do that since, more often than not, it's women who expect men to read their minds rather than the other way around.

Once you've settled on your preferences (or differing levels of dislike), schedule your chores and activities with the baby. Don't set this in stone, though. Sometimes, you may want to switch for a particular day or time. Build this into the schedule if you have to. It may also be useful to do the same duties on different days, so one of you cleans up on Mondays and Wednesdays, the other on Tuesdays and Thursdays, and both of you relax from Friday to Sunday.

If one of you is too OCD to let the place get messy for the weekend, then that person should clean up. If that person is your wife, you should help. However, you should try to persuade her that, until baby becomes a teenager, a messy home will be part of life. (When they become a teenager, then their messy room will be part of life.) If, by chance, you are the neatnik, then you need to let go of your need for order so your partner can stay sane.

If you can afford it, hire a cleaner to come in twice a week or whatever level of dirt you can tolerate.

Lastly, always keep the schedule open for updates.

Taboo topics

For the first few months, most of your conversation, directly and otherwise, will be about baby. Partly because your partner is likely to be oversensitive at this time, you should avoid letting your unguarded mouth get you in trouble. Here are three topics you'll either want to avoid treat with the utmost delicacy:

1. *What happened in the delivery room.* Unless everything went according to plan, don't talk about how the birth went. In fact, even if everything did go according to plan, still don't talk about it. She might be thinking she should have had a different birth plan, and she might be blaming herself if her birth plan went awry.

Either way, if you must refer to it, just tell her she did well.

2. *Breast or bottle.* The message that breast is best is all around but, as with so many personal issues, the science is not settled[7]. But, even if it was, your partner is the one feeding, and she is best placed to decide what's best for baby and her and, yes, you as well—breast milk only, formula only, or a combination of both. After all, other considerations come into play, such as time and energy and returning to work.

3. *Don't talk about work unless she brings it up.* That means: don't talk about her work or yours. She may be fretting about returning because now she sees her most important job as being a mother. Or she may be worrying about how soon she can return to work because she's already getting cabin fever and there are bills to pay. And you should avoid telling her about what's going on in the office in case she feels like you're out there in the world while she's trapped at home. Bottom line: take all your cues from her on this topic.

How to argue nicely

No matter how hard you try, you're going to have disagreements. Don't try to avoid them or, worse, suppress them. That only makes things worse down the line. Instead, use the following ground rules to ensure arguments don't get out of hand and have productive outcomes:

- Don't criticize your partner—instead, make a suggestion. For example, don't say, "Why do you always forget to get more baby wipes?" but rather say, "Let me know when we're running low on wipes so I can get more."
- If you do forget and criticize or insult or get snarky, apologize.
- Ask her how she's feeling.
- If your partner is criticizing you (or even being insulting), paraphrase what she says and ask if you're accurately expressing what she said. Once she agrees, then, if you think she's wrong or unfair, rebut her accusation. This is more effective because you've already shown that you took the time to understand what she's saying.
- Don't go on and on, though. Say what you have to briefly and let your partner respond.

- Avoid the temptation to score points. If your partner says you didn't wash the dishes properly, don't say, "Well, I hardly have any clean clothes because you haven't done the laundry in weeks." Instead, focus on how both of you can solve the problem.
- If none of this works and tempers start to flare, walk away. Only when you've both cooled down, then you continue.
- Ensure your partner has no other concerns before closing off the conversation[8].

Five topics you *should* talk about

You and your partner's parental expectations are a discussion you should have before baby comes but, if you forgot that in the excitement about becoming parents, it's certainly something you should delve into deeply before baby starts talking. The key issues here are:

- Discipline
- Routine
- Education
- Diet
- Relatives

Following the same rules for arguing nicely listed above, you and your partner should come to an agreement on all these topics (and discuss each in excruciating detail. Two good effects come from this: first, you will feel like you're working together to do what is best for your family and, two, by coming to a consensus on these issues, you get baby out of your headspace and have more bandwidth to focus on each other.

So, regarding discipline, talk about what methods each of you prefers to use when your child is naughty or rude or throws a tantrum. What will be the routine for bedtime and for meals? What kind of school do you want to send them to, and how much homework is too much? Will they be allowed to have snacks before they're five and, if so, what kind and at what times? How much access should grandparents, aunties, and uncles have? If you are adherents of different faiths, will you want to raise a baby to believe in the Ohio State Buckeyes or the Alabama Crimson Tide?

Couple Time

Once baby's old enough (and even before, if you have grandparents or trusted friends who are willing to babysit), you and your partner should go out on dates. Or just a walk. The important thing here is to connect like you did before baby came. You might even want to make it a rule to have no baby talk while you're out. Talk about grown-up stuff, like the state of the economy, the history of corn, and whether Scotch tape was made by the same people who invented whiskey. It's also helpful to discuss how you see your future, your ambitions, and your dreams and how you will each share in them.

Check-ins keep you both balanced

If, as usually happens, you return to work before she does, make sure to call home a few times a day. But make sure she's okay with this. It may be best to have set times for calling so you don't interrupt her nap or some other activity. When the two of you are back out to work, keep up this practice. You presumably had a good relationship before, or else you wouldn't have had a child, so it's important now to do more of what you did before to keep your relationship strong. Regular communication also helps you know better when your partner may be feeling stressed or discontented.

The King Solomon solution

Divide the baby. Mothers often fall into two categories —those who never want to let go of baby because they made this miraculous creature and mothers who get overwhelmed and need time without baby duties. In either situation, you need to have a deep discussion with your partner about balancing baby time. If she's possessive, gently cajole her into giving you exclusive time with baby, pointing out all the things she can do with her free time, like bathing. If she's overwhelmed, take the baby for as long as you can but specify how long beforehand so that *you* don't feel taken advantage of.

How did we make this baby again?

In case you're wondering—and you are—it takes about <u>seven weeks on average</u> for couples to resume having sex after baby comes. But the average doesn't matter—how soon you and your partner start back knocking boots is between you, her, and the little creature who has her too tired to even roll over.

Still, rarin' as you might be to go, you need to bear a few things in mind: (1) you didn't carry around 25-plus extra pounds for several months, (2) you didn't push six to eight of those pounds out of your body through the same aperture that had previously fitted your penis, and (3) your nipples haven't changed from erogenous zones to drinking tubes.

Which is to say, you have to wait until she's ready. However, that doesn't prevent you from trying to nudge her closer to that desired time. Here are some suggestions for beginning that campaign:

The forgotten art of seduction

Here's the problem: your partner is less likely to want sex than you. That's generally the case with men and women, even without a baby. After all, most men only need to see a smile and a boob to get turned on. (And admit it, we don't care that her boobs are full of milk. We only care that she has bigger ones now.) Women, however, need foreplay to get in the mood, like their spouse making them *pâté de foie gras.* "You need to understand that after being peed on, pooped on and puked on by this little baby, your partner probably doesn't feel very sexy," says Ian Kerner, a relationship expert and author of *Love in the Time of Colic: The New Parents Guide to Getting It On Again.* "Because so much of female sexual desire comes down to self-esteem, it's important to help her restore a sense of sanity[9]."

So, if you're not a professional chef, clean the house, change the sheets, and shave her legs. (Yes, I know you don't care, but she does.)

Remember the bases

Even if you and she aren't ready for what former President Bill Clinton called "sexual relations," you can still try a Monica Lewinsky. Proceed like you did in high school when you were trying to get to first base— if you can remember those hormone-saturated days. Offer her a back massage and see what happens from there. Or, better yet, a foot rub because, in case you didn't know, the part of the brain that gets signals from the feet is right next to the part of the brain that gets signals from our genitals. Try playing with her toes. If you do it right, your piggy may get to run *aaalll* the way home.

Don't expect what you're expecting

Finally, be prepared for the sex to be different. It may be because she's not comfortable with her post-pregnant body or a myriad of other reasons. You yourself might not be at your best. That may be because of tiredness or even because you now see your partner in the new role of mother as well as lover. At the other extreme, she may want to spice up your sex life now that you two are back in the saddle again. Who knows? She might even ask you to buy a saddle.

GIVE OTHER DADS THE PEACE OF KNOWING THAT THEY ARE THE BEST DAD FOR THEIR CHILD.

You have now honed crucial skills such as helping your partner stay healthy during her pregnancy, acing daddy's vital duties when your baby's born, helping your baby enjoy a peaceful night's slumber, and so much more.

Simply by leaving your honest opinion of this book on Amazon, you'll show other dads a plethora of practical and personal skills that will empower them to feel more confident as new fathers.

Thank you for your help. You can encourage other fathers to discover the caring, nurturing, loving dad they hold within.

Scan the QR code for a quick review!

CONCLUSION

I'm not boasting when I say that this is the only book you will need to read as a new dad. That's because the best thing you can do for your infant child is provide for their basic needs. This is what you've learned to do from these pages. You now know everything you need to know about pregnancy, helping your partner while she's pregnant and in the delivery room, what to do when the baby comes, how to nurture your baby, and how to keep your romance alive after you become a dad (even if you get a dad bod).

Many baby websites, parenting books, and even scientific studies will say you need to do a lot more than that. They tell you that, to ensure your child is healthy and emotionally well-adjusted and successful in school, they should sleep this way, eat that way, and be parented in a particular style, and so on. According to all these experts, parenting is a nonstop job where you must always be on high alert and follow expert guidance to the letter if you don't want your child to become an alcoholic high school dropout divorcee with heart disease.

Ignore them.

I'll say it for the last time: you and your partner are the experts on your child. If the professional experts say something that contradicts your experience, go with what you believe is best for your baby.

Yes, you will make mistakes, but you will make even more by trying to follow the advice of all these parenting gurus. Apart from the basic care laid out in this book, there is no one-size-fits-all approach to parenting. Most importantly, trying to do everything right removes the joy of being a parent and turns you into a guardian forever worrying about doing something that will traumatize your child for life.

The incontrovertible fact is that the only people who were traumatized for life by their childhood were those who grew up under conditions of war, famine, or extreme abuse over many years. And even many of them overcame their traumas with the right kind of help.

Economist Bryan Caplan puts it like this: "The best available evidence shows that large differences in upbringing have little effect on how kids turn out. While healthy, smart, happy, successful virtuous parents tend to have matching offspring, the reason is largely nature, not nurture[1]."

What this means is that a large part of your children's future outcomes has been decided even before they were born through your genetic contribution (and your partner's) to their DNA. On top of that, much of their socialization will happen outside the home because it's the world they must grapple with as adults, not Dad and Mom. And, since they're living in a First World nation, they're more likely to grapple successfully.

The takeaway here is to take joy in your child, knowing that once you provide them with food, shelter, clothing, and a tablet, they will be fine. But, you may be wondering, if what you do as a parent makes little difference in your child's future, what's your role as a parent?

Well, I saw the answer to that at the birthday celebration we had for Ashley when she turned two. I invited Roger, my college friend I mentioned in the Introduction, who I consulted for father advice. He came with his wife and their two children, a ten-year-old boy and an eight-year-old girl.

"So, it turned out to be not as scary as originally thought?" he said as we sat watching the children play.

I laughed. "It was scarier, but not for the reasons I thought."

He grinned. "It's worth it, though," he said.

He looked across at his children, who were focused on their tablets, and, as if sensing their daddy's gaze, they looked up at him simultaneously. He smiled, and they smiled back. The love between them was as natural as gravity.

In that moment, I understood what kind of future I should strive for as a dad. I understood then that being a parent is not a role—it's a relationship. And it's what you are now and for the rest of your life. Having a baby is, in itself, a life-changing experience.

As you already know (or will soon find out), to see yourself as a dad means a permanent change in the identity or identities you had before. Also, caring for a child enriches your life and your character. This book has, I hope, helped prepare you for the practical challenges of that important relationship. (If you agree, please leave a review on Amazon and/or Good Reads.)

Remember that you don't need to be perfect—your love for your child will make you the best parent you can be.

Even the mistakes you will inevitably make will help you become better and better each day. Don't be hard on yourself. You can make it one step at a time.

Parenting is an adventure that never ends. As you watch your baby become a toddler, your toddler become a child, your child become a teenager, and then a young adult, your constant goal is to nurture your relationship with your baby—because, in your heart of hearts, that's what they will always be. You also change as a parent with each stage because your child will have different needs as they grow older. You have to figure out how much to let go so they can learn to stand on their own feet more and more until, when they are all grown up, they are, hopefully, ready to face the world and create their own space within it.

You will always love them, no matter what and, when they are children, they will return that love just as absolutely. That love will always connect you and, when they are grown and have children of their own, then they will truly understand and appreciate what you did for them as their dad.

NOTES

INTRODUCTION

1. Murkoff and Mazell, p. 472.
2. Raeburn 2014, p. 5.
3. Medina 2014, p. 58.

1. START WITH SUPPORT

1. verywellmind. "Stages of Prenatal Development." Kendra Cherry and Carly Snyder, MD. June 1, 2020.
2. What to Expect When You're Expecting, p. 538.
3. Insta Father. "Why Dads Should Embrace Childbirth Class, plus 10 Things to Look for When Choosing a Baby Prep Course." 28/07/15.
4. What To Expect. "How to Create a Birth Plan." Jennifer Kelly Geddes and Oluwatosin Goje, M.D. 17/06/21.
5. verywellfamily. "Everything You Need for Your Newborn Baby." Wendy Wisner. November 29, 2022.
6. BPAS. "Breastfeeding and formula feeding." Accessed 02/02/23.
7. Social Science & Medicine. "Is breast truly best?" Volume 109, May 2014, pp. 55-65.
8. American Academy of Pediatrics. "Updates Safe Sleep Recommendations: Back is Best." 21/06/22.
9. Parenting Without Borders. Christine Gross-Loh. Penguin, 2013., p. 16.
10. bellybelly. "15 Great Ways to Support Her During Pregnancy." July 19, 2022.

2. HELPING HER STAY HEALTHY
DURING PREGNANCY

1. KidsHealth. "Medical Care During Pregnancy." Thinh Phu Nguyen, MD, July 2022.
2. Centers for Disease Control and Prevention. "Data & Statistics on Birth Defects." December 21, 2022.
3. Ultrasound in Obstetrics and Gynecology. "Ultrasound in pregnancy and non-right handedness: meta-analysis of randomized trials." K. Å. Salvesen. May 16, 2011.
4. KidsHealth. "Rh Incompatibility During Pregnancy." Thinh Phu Nguyen, MD. July 2022.
5. National Institutes of Health. "NIH study links morning sickness to lower risk of pregnancy loss." September 26, 2016.
6. Better Health Channel. "Pregnancy and exercise." **Pregnancy and exercise - Better Health Channel.** Accessed 07/02/23.

3. HOW TO SUPPORT YOUR PARTNER
DURING LABOR AND DELIVERY

1. History News Network. "How Did Men End Up in the Delivery Room?" Judith Walzer Leavitt. Accessed February 13, 2023.
2. Cochrane. "Continuous support for women during childbirth." Accessed February 13, 2023.
3. bellybelly. "Hospital Birth Classes Are Sabotaging Women's Birth Plans, Say Midwives. Kelly Winder. August 11, 2022.
4. bellybelly. "9 Ways Independent Birth Classes Can Help You Get Better Results." Kelly Winder. July 12, 2022.
5. Cochrane. "Continuous support for women during childbirth." Accessed February 13, 2023.
6. National Library of Medicine. "Continuous support for women during childbirth." Ellen D Hodnett, Simon Gates, G Justus Hofmeyr, Carol Sakala. October 17, 2012.

4. AFTER CHILDBIRTH: PROVIDING FOR YOUR BABY'S NEEDS

1. KQED. "New DNA Studies Debunk Misconceptions About Paternal Relationships." Barry Starr, November 25, 2013.
2. Ars Technica. "Cuckoldry is incredibly rare among humans." Annalee Newitz, May 4, 2016.
3. artofmanliness. "A Man's Guide to Pregnancy." Brett & Kate McKay. May 30, 2021.
4. Warwick University. "Research punctures 'modern' fathers myth - except for nappies that is . . ." Accessed February 20, 2022
5. What to Expect. "How to Bathe Your Newborn Baby." Jennifer Kelly Geddes and Gina Posner. November 2, 2021.
6. Psychological Science. "Five-Month-Old Infants Have General Knowledge of How Nonsolid Substances Behave and Interact." Susan J. Hespos et al. Volume 7, Issue 2. January 7, 2016.
7. National Institute of Health. "Speech and Language Developmental Milestones." NIH Publication No. 13-4781, September 2010.
8. babycenter. "Age-by-age guide to feeding your baby." Dana Dubinsky and Erin Hinga. February 8, 2022.
9. babycenter. "Foods that can be unsafe for your baby." Karen Niles and Erin Hinga. February 9, 2022.
10. Children's Hospital of Philadelphia. "The Truth about Peanut Allergies in Kids." April 10, 2018.
11. Aeon. "The marvel of the human dad." Anna Machin. January 17, 2019.

5. SLEEP TRAINING YOUR BABY

1. William C. Dement and Christopher Vaughan. *The Promise of Sleep*. Dell Publishing, 1999. p. 231.
2. Johns Hopkins Medicine. "New Parents: Tips for Quality Rest." Accessed February 28, 2023.

3. Bluebell. "The importance of sleep in your baby's first year." Accessed February 28, 2023.

4. Psychological Science. S Scarr, D Phillips, K McCartney. "Facts, Fantasies and the Future of Child Care in the United States." Vol 1, Issue 1, 1990.

5. What to Expect. "How to Sleep Train Your Baby." Colleen de Bellefonds and Jesil Pazhayampallil, M.D., F.A.A.P. February 17, 2022.

6. BabyCenter. "Baby sleep training: When and how to start." Colleen de Bellefonds and Chandani DeZure, M.D. May 31, 2022.

7. What to Expect. "Cry It Out Method of Sleep Training." Colleen de Bellefonds and Kyle Monk, M.D. February 24, 2022.

8. Dement and Vaughan, p. 401.

9. What to Expect. "What Is the Ferber Method of Sleep Training?" Marygrace Taylor and Kyle Monk, M.D. February 24, 2022.

10. What to Expect. "Using the Chair Method of Sleeping Training to Get Your Baby to Sleep." Jennifer Kelly Geddes and Gina Posner, M.D. June 9, 2022.

11. Pampers Smart Sleep Coach. "Pick Up, Put Down Sleep Training: How to Start." Mandy Treeby. Feb 16th, 2023.

6. BONDING WITH YOUR BABY: HELPING THEM DEVELOP THEIR MENTAL AND EMOTIONAL HEALTH

1. Christine Gross-Loh. Parenting Without Borders, 2013. p. 217.

2. The Gottman Institute. "An Age-By-Age Guide to Helping Kids Manage Emotions." Sanya Pelini. Accessed March 2, 2023.

3. Human Development. "Theorizing the Father-Child Relationship: Mechanisms and Developmental Outcomes." Daniel Paquette. August, 2004.

4. Baby360. "The Importance of Father-Infant Bonding Time." Aug 10, 2016

5. National Library of Medicine. "Meta-analysis of the heritability of human traits based on fifty years of twin studies." Polderman, Benyamin, de Leeuw et al. July, 2015.

6. Parents ®. "12 Ways for Dad to Bond with Baby." Kaelin Zawilin-ski. May 31, 2009.

7. Lamaze International. "11 Ways Dads Can Bond with Baby Right Away." Cara Terreri. June 14, 2019.

8. European Journal of Psychology of Education. "Fathers' influences on children's development: The evidence from two-parent families." Michael E. Lamb and Charlies Lewis, 2003.

9. Scientific American. "The Serious Need for Play." Melinda Wenner Moyer. February-March, 2009.

10. Forest School Association. "New Research – A Longitudinal Study on Forest School." Dave Brooks. February 1, 2019.

11. Workopolis. "5 work-life balance tips for new working dads." June 16, 2017.

12. World Economic Forum. "Which countries spend the most time on social media?" April 29, 2022.

13. The Australian Parenting Website. "Mental health for babies and toddlers." Accessed March 3, 2023.

7. KEEPING YOUR ROMANTIC RELATIONSHIP STRONG

1. Marriage and Family Living. "Parenthood as crisis." E.E. LeMasters. November, 1957.

2. Journal of Family Psychology. "The Baby and the Marriage." Alyson Fearniey Shapiro, John M. Gottman et al. 2000.

3. John Medina. *Brain Rules for Baby*, 2014. p. 80.

4. Jordan Peterson. *Beyond Order: 12 More Rules for Life.* Portfolio, 2021, loc. 3911 (e-book).

5. Parents ®. "7 Common Marriage Issues After Baby and How to Solve Them." Charlie Sumner and Suzanne Schlosberg. January 5, 2023.

6. BabyCenter. "Dividing childcare and housework duties with your partner." Linda Murray. Accessed March 4, 2023.

7. National Library of Medicine. "Improved Estimates of the Benefits of Breastfeeding Using Sibling Comparisons to Reduce Selection Bias." Eirik Evenhouse and Siobhan Reilly. December 5, 2005.

8. Parents ®. "7 Common Marriage Issues After Baby and How to Solve Them." Charlie Sumner and Suzanne Schlosberg. January 5, 2023.

9. Parents ®. "A Dad's Guide to Sex After Baby." Matt Villano. May 17, 2022.

CONCLUSION

1. Bryan Caplan. Selfish Reasons to Have More Kids. Basic Books, 2011, p. 34.

Made in the USA
Columbia, SC
14 December 2024

49420727R00096